Wilma Kirsten has been in clinical practice since 2005 and holds two honours science degrees, one in Nutritional Therapy and the other in Molecular Cell Biology and Health Sciences. She specialises in digestive disorders (IBS and IBD) and female hormonal well-being (PMS and menopause) and has successfully helped hundreds of patients address symptoms of ill health in her clinic. In addition to her busy practice, Wilma acts as Consultant Nutritionist for The Musical Theatre Academy (MTA) in London. From 2009 to 2014, Wilma fulfilled the role of Expert Nutrition Columnist for *Positive Health Online* magazine.

To the three scientists in my life who help me stay true to
facts and statistics.

# Wilma Kirsten

# IDEAL PLATE COMPOSITION

## CHOOSE FOOD TO HELP YOU BE YOUR BEST SELF

AUSTIN MACAULEY PUBLISHERS™

LONDON • CAMBRIDGE • NEW YORK • SHARJAH

A CIP catalogue record for this title is available from the British Library.

ISBN 9781528907019 (Paperback)
ISBN 9781528907026 (Kindle e-book)
ISBN 9781528958462 (ePub e-book)

www.austinmacauley.com

First Published (2019)
Austin Macauley Publishers Ltd
25 Canada Square
Canary Wharf
London
E14 5LQ

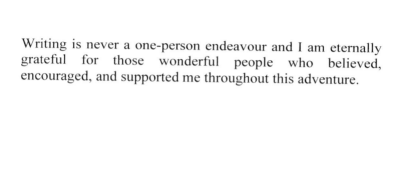

Writing is never a one-person endeavour and I am eternally grateful for those wonderful people who believed, encouraged, and supported me throughout this adventure.

# Table of Contents

# Foreword

The book you are holding may turn out to be one of the most important books you have read. Books related to health and healthy eating are abound and there are many good books one could read. But too many are either too academic or make unfounded claims based on wishful thinking. This book strikes an excellent balance, distilling scientific research and clinical experience spanning many years into a very approachable format. The core message of this book is easy to understand and together with the supporting knowledge you will learn, it will allow you to incorporate and maintain changes in your diet that will have long-lasting effects. These changes, as you will see in the vignettes presenting a person in each chapter, can make a huge difference to your health and mental state.

There are many things that contribute to our wellbeing, and these can be seen to fall broadly into the three categories of physiological, psychological, and social. Food and eating occupy all three categories and, whilst nothing is a panacea, Wilma proposes the one thing that can affect all three and is likely to benefit everyone, regardless of what ails them.

There are things that are necessary for survival and things that contribute to our well-being. Sufficient oxygen, temperatures within a fairly narrow range, water, and food are all required to survive. Lack of oxygen or extreme temperatures will result in a quick demise, lack of water will take a few days, and lack of food is likely to result in an untimely death in weeks. On the other hand, a safe environment, friendship, intimate relationships, validation, and good nutrition are all things that contribute to our well-being, even if a lack of them would not necessarily be life-threatening.

As you may have noticed, food falls into both categories. It is essential for us to eat or we will starve, but it is also important that we eat food that will nourish us if we want to be well. Even if we ignore the social and psychological aspect of food and eating, we can see that it occupies a unique place in our quest for health.

Necessary requirements are, if met, mostly ignored by us. Unless we often suffer from lack of oxygen, are exposed regularly to extreme temperatures or states of severe dehydration, the psychology is fairly simple and can be described in terms of homoeostasis, the way an organism strives to maintain a state of balance. If temperatures drop, we employ physiological and behavioural strategies to maintain our core temperature. Arrector pili contract to warm us up, we move out of the elements, wear warmer clothes, start a fire, and possibly even decrease blood flow to the extremities to maintain our core temperature. The key point here is that, from a psychological point of view, unless we are physically threatened, the maintenance of homoeostasis is almost totally unnoticed.

As nutrients are very important for many physiological functions, it is sensible to wonder whether our appetites are driven by homoeostasis too. You may have come across the belief that, if you feel like something, it is possibly because your body is telling you to replenish some nutrient or other. It is appealing to think that we crave that chocolate because it contains magnesium and we are probably deficient. Much of the early research into the psychology of eating followed this thought process, starting with a basic homeostasis of glucose or lipids and progressively getting more sophisticated. The fundamental problem with assuming that we seek foods that replenish the nutrients that we need is the sheer number of nutrients required for optimal health and the variation in nutrient content in the foods we eat. This approach is still proposed by some people because it 'makes sense' and they may even present supporting evidence in research. Some research seemed to support the homeostatic principle as a driver for what we eat where, for example, rats fed on a diet lacking an essential amino acid got sick and later showed a preference for a food containing the nutrient. The homeostatic interpretation was that the rats were seeking food containing what they were deficient in and there was this internal wisdom guiding them to the correct nutrition. This interpretation was refuted by further, similar experiments where either presenting a new, deficient food, or two new foods (one deficient and one not) clearly showed that the rats avoided the food that had made them sick, but they had no preference for the food containing the nutrient they were lacking. The rats had merely learnt that the one food was not making them feel well and thus avoided it. The key point here is that, whilst appealing, the idea that you feel like a certain type of food because there is some ingredient in it that your body needs is not supported by any research. If you feel like something you might benefit from the enjoyment it brings but do not try to justify it as somehow nutritionally beneficial.

Food avoidance is very common and at times we develop very strong dislikes for foods. The strongest of these aversions are those related to foods that were consumed shortly before experiencing nausea or strong gastrointestinal discomfort. One such incident suffices for us to avoid a particular food for the rest of our lives. Most people have a food that they have a strong aversion to because of a single experience and most readers will be able to think of the food and the experience without too much difficulty. This strong aversion makes sense as we would associate these foods with toxicity and thus avoidance of these would be a strong adaptive trait in our evolution. A quick diversion into the concept of psychological conditioning will help us better understand the drivers and mental processes behind this strong aversion.

Conditioning in psychology can be traced all the way back to the famous studies by Pavlov with dogs. The dogs had associated a bell with the imminent arrival of food and started displaying physiological signs of preparing for a meal as soon as they heard the bell. Classical conditioning describes how a response, in this case, the increased salivation and production of gastric juices, is conditioned by a recurring stimulus, the bell.

Repeating the stimulus just before the meal arrived resulted in the dogs responding a certain way even if the food was not presented. This type of conditioning does not fit the food avoidance described above as it requires multiple exposures to a stimulus before the response is conditioned and attenuates over time i.e. if, over a period, the bell no longer preceded the arrival of food, the response would slowly diminish until it was extinguished and the dogs would no longer react to the stimulus.

Food aversion requires one stimulus and may remain for the rest of our lives and could be explained at least to some extent by operant conditioning. Operant conditioning requires a more active role by the participant such as a bird or rat requiring to press a lever to receive a reward. The animal associates the lever press with the arrival of the reward and so the conditioning occurs. Although traditionally operant conditioning also requires multiple exposures, nausea and gastrointestinal symptoms are strong enough for us to form a link between the food and the illness. The maintenance of the conditioning is done by actively avoiding the food; eschewing and not experiencing the symptoms goes a long way to reinforce the idea that the food should be avoided. Even in the simple case where there is a direct, easily explainable, reason for us to steer away from a food, our active participation in the maintenance of this aversion is evident. Imagine how much more our mindset and approach to food affects what we are prepared to eat and what we are not.

Aversion to food is not only towards foods that have made us ill in the past but also linked with strong food dislikes. Research is unequivocal about how exposure to certain flavours, right from the time we are a foetus, affects our likes and dislikes in later life. The more flavours we experience earlier on, the more likely we are to enjoy a more varied diet later in life. Expanding the type of foods we enjoy can be challenging for many people and it does take effort, perseverance, and a lot of reflection on what we are experiencing. Human beings, like other mammals, tend to be neophobic when it comes to food. We know from research that rats will only consume a small amount of a new food and will increase consumption only once they do not experience any ill side-effects. A very sensible strategy to ensure they are not poisoned by unknown food.

Humans, although much more complex than rats, are very similar. New things are avoided by many, especially if these new things have a strong flavour, unfamiliar texture, or even look odd to us. Unfortunately, when someone does not like vegetables, introducing them requires concerted effort and reflection on the whole process. On the positive side, research shows that having something we do not like reduces our aversion to it. The more we are exposed to something the less likely we are to dislike it. Furthermore, if a food is paired with a food we like, we tend to start liking the other food as well. This means that a good strategy would be to introduce a small quantity of a vegetable we do not like together with one that we do enjoy and slowly increase the portion of the vegetable we had previously avoided. Take time to reflect on what is happening when you try these foods and not only will you discover that you are actually enjoying a wider variety of things, but you will probably learn quite a lot about yourself.

To further understand how we have acquired our food preferences we now look at how our social environment and culture affect our attitudes toward food. Certainly, our immediate social environment, our kith and kin, determine the flavours and foods we are exposed to from an early age and strongly affects our palate's 'palette' in the way we discussed above. But there are more factors at play and attitudes towards food are built up over the years and learnt from the people we interact with. As an Italian, I am very much aware of how unadventurous most of my compatriots are, using the 'Italian is the best food in the world' excuse to avoid sampling any foreign muck. I remember talking to someone who found the English idea of bacon and eggs for breakfast disgusting. All this whilst tucking into a focaccia farcita which, to the uninitiated, is basically bread with raw bacon. Yes, this was at breakfast. Clearly, either choice of the first meal of the day can be derided by many people, even before we look at the nutritional value of either. Hopefully, you can see that without reflecting on how we are behaving, it is too easy to exclude foods based on cultural biases.

Cultural influences and frequent exposure also colours and reinforces our tendency to eat the same foods. I have come across untold people who, having grown up with food that is spicy, find non-spicy food too bland. Many Italians cannot live without bread or pasta for longer than two meals. I recently met a couple in Japan where the husband was sick of rice and fish and needed a proper meal of steak and fries – they had arrived the day before and this was their third meal in Japan.

The list is interminable but the underlying drivers behind these very strong preferences, bordering on addiction, are many. Pasta and white bread are a small step away from pure sugar and so have the obvious physiological effects of a glycaemic spike. White rice and white maize meal are not much different. But, very importantly, most of the food we consume in a familiar environment is consumed within a positive emotional context. Whether it is the spiciness from the capsaicin in chilli peppers, the complex flavour of a mole poblano, or just a plate of pasta in front of you, eating in a relaxed environment nourishes our body and our soul.

At the physiological level, we go from hunger to satiation, but the best meals are those where we have had time to prepare for and find ourselves in a safe and nurturing environment. Our bodies, much in the same way that Pavlov's dogs' did, get ready in anticipation of the food that we will eat. It has been observed that we produce *cephalic insulin* in anticipation of a meal rich in carbohydrates i.e. our body will produce insulin even before we have taken the first bite of our calorie dense refined carbohydrate hit. It does this to mitigate the inevitable glycaemic spike that the food will induce and is a very useful trait, but by no means the only one that prepares us for our food. Olfactory cues, the time of day, the attitude of the people around you, and possibly even setting the table all are conducive to many imperceptible changes in the body that allows us to assimilate our food in an optimal way. If we have the privilege of being able to experience a relaxed, convivial meal with our nearest and dearest, we should grab the opportunity with both hands as often as possible. These meals are nourishing in every possible way and the more we see their value, the more valuable they will be to us.

Wilma's book will provide you with all the information you need to change your diet, food habits and enjoyment of food, but it will challenge you. It will require that you engage in the process, that you get to know what dislikes are holding you back and that you overcome those hurdles. If you are one of the fortunate few who love food in all its guises and enjoy an inclusive, varied diet, the journey will be easy. If you are not, you are one of the fortunate ones who have the unique opportunity of being the agent in changes that will transform your world of food. You will discover much about yourself and will experience the joys of a truly inclusive diet. This newfound curiosity about food and the opportunity to experience new things is one of life's greatest pleasures. Feeling great after a meal is an added bonus.

Do give this book a chance, follow its suggestions and learn from it. Engage with the preparation of the food, the ceremony of sharing a meal, and the experience of eating each food. This is *your* experience and your time, may it be well spent.

**S. Salvi, MBPsS**

# Preface

I talk about food a lot, too much apparently. According to my friends and family, I eat only healthy meals (and they make it their mission to show me what I am missing out on). They are wrong, of course: despite my nutritional focus, I have my favourite indulgences, which would make a purist shudder. I have a very positive relationship with food, which has been cemented by my life experience and my early exposure to all things edible. I grew up in a household at a time when mealtimes were sacred. I was one of those children who had a cutlery set with my name on the spoon, fork, and knife; I also had a plate with the same engraving. Most of our meals were enjoyed in the kitchen, by the oval table with the plastic, easy to wipe, tablecloth. The crockery was hefty, durable, and a memorable dark plum colour. It was not a designer Wedgwood but a treasured gift from my godmother to her favourite niece, my mother. It still takes centre stage in the cupboard, 40 years after making its first appearance.

My father works with local farmers and some of them still pay him with produce, particularly meat: good quality grain-fed beef, and sometimes lamb. Our main meal of the day could not have been more traditional if my mother had written the New World food manifesto. I loved every bite of succulent meat, grain of white rice, and green beans, sweet potato, or carrot. Fridays were fish days, haddock or hake with homemade fries, and a side serving of freshly cut tomato wedges and cucumber slices. Pure heaven. Apart from the occasional boxed cereal at breakfast, my upbringing was focused around real food, the stuff our ancestors hunted and gathered. For me, the word 'food' conjures up a cacophony of emotions, memories, and images.

For some people the associations are less positive; often that is due in part to financial constraints or lack of availability; more often though, it is due to a lack of skill and interest in preparing meals. Many people view food as anything edible, be it an apple or a triple chocolate chip cookie. To paraphrase George Orwell, all foods are equal, but some foods are more equal than others. The world of human nutrition is evolving rapidly; to fully grasp the science behind the advice, we must ensure that we are not influenced by exuberant bloggers, flashy website graphics, or prime-time advertisements. My personal favourite examples are those advertisements that state that in no time at all I can both lose weight and discover the real me, just by eating a particular breakfast cereal, yoghurt, or butter substitute. Clearly, the look I desire is that of the slim models having the time of their lives as they strut through an immaculately manicured park, or unveil their radiant, whiter-than-white pearly smiles.

We cite a lack of time as one of the main reasons that we cannot cook, exercise, or sleep properly. We attribute our rapacious appetites for ready meals, take-outs, and lunch-time sandwiches to our frenetic lifestyles. Our careers engulf all our energy, and the success they bring allows us to finance a lifestyle that is far removed from that of our forefathers.

When Homo sapiens roamed the plains, foraging for food was the number one priority (closely followed by avoiding being a food source for some other species). Either you found food, or you risked starvation. Today, we spend so much time and effort on distancing ourselves from our food, as far as possible; we distance ourselves from the nutritious food that goes straight from the land to the table, perhaps with a little washing, slicing, dicing, and cooking in between. We have become addicted to processed food. For a significant amount of people, food is only deemed suitable for consumption when it has undergone a number of transitional steps. From Twinkies to tequila, if all I have to do is unwrap it or uncork it to experience an oral taste sensation which is worthy of a Tweet or an Instagram post, then my nurturing is complete.

Many people believe that with the right amount of money, and a bit of luck, their unavoidable appointment with death will be delayed. Linda McCartney was slim and a vegetarian, in stark contrast to Luciano Pavarotti who was majestic in stature and an omnivore. Linda died aged 56, and Luciano aged 71; cancer took them both. Ronnie Wood, an alcoholic, fathered twin girls on the 1 June 2016, aged 68; despite allegedly checking himself into rehab six times for alcohol addiction, he is still going strong. Linda, an animal activist, wrote several vegetarian cookbooks and championed her own range of vegetarian dishes. She clearly paid attention to her food choices and reconciled it with her passion for animal welfare. From the looks of it, Luciano (one of the most commercially successful tenors of all times) ate with gusto. Ronnie is often humorously referred to as the rocker who defies death at all cost, especially compared with the myriad of much-loved celebrities that passed away prematurely in 2016.

On the other side of the English Channel, in a town called Arles situated on the southern tip of France, Jeanne Louise Calment passed away at the age of 122 years and 164 days on the 4 August 1997. I think it is safe to say that Jeanne died of old age, given that she has been given the title of 'the longest confirmed human lifespan on record'. Her life's journey started on the 21 February 1875, in the same town where she died (she never moved away). She did not have to work after the age of 21, because of her husband's income as a shop owner. Reportedly, she occupied her time with hobbies, including fencing, tennis and playing the piano. Her longer-than-average life was not without tragedy: her only daughter died from pneumonia, aged 36; her one, and only, grandson shockingly perished in an automobile accident when he too was only 36. Jeanne publicly announced that she was never ill during her expansive life and many people reported on her obvious love of sweets. This formidable lady, weighing a mere 40 kg (88 pounds) stood at only 137 cm (4 foot 6 inches) in her slippers; yet apparently, she would eat over 1 kg (2.2 pounds) of chocolate in a single week more than once in the latter stages of her remarkably long life.

Examples like these make it seem like your life-expectancy really is random; as if all we really need to worry about is short-term. We slew dangerous animals, sailed the seven seas, and deforested the jungle (or at least our ancestors did); now we desire the picture-perfect lifestyle because modern technology has gifted us a plethora of time-saving devices, which require a mere voice-activating command or the flick of a switch. That elusive way of life (you know, the one that looks so good in Country House, Forbes Rich list, and Vogue) is *surely* achievable, without even ruining a French manicure. We seem to have an insatiable appetite for the next and best magic formula which will help us achieve these goals. When it comes to making sure that they live life to the full, it appears that human beings (in certain geographical areas) will try almost anything. Anything, that is, that does not require much effort.

Here in the West, we no longer battle famine, contaminated water, or large scale parasitic infectious diseases. For many of us, the greatest struggles are beating the rush hour traffic to make it home for the weekly delivery of groceries, enduring A&E waiting times when we cut our fingers separating frozen hamburgers with a kitchen knife, and making sure that we have enough tequila to finish the night's festivities properly. Most importantly, we struggle to look fabulous whilst we do it all. From washboard abs to flawless skin, we *deserve* it.

We want to shed the extra pounds of body weight by embarking on a mere 15-minute workout per day: the less time tensing, flexing, and stretching, the better. We embark on any diet that promises instant weight loss (if we even subscribe to the idea that what you eat does actually make a difference). No sacrifice is too large, just so long as the benefits are instant; if noticeable results take more than a month, then we simply move on to the latest wonder cure/diet/workout. If the current best thing is surgery, then we will slip on that backless gown and hop on the gurney – if we can get the health insurance company or NHS to pay for it. Surely, bariatric surgery is easier than changing our life-long questionable eating habits. Evidently, it is far better to spend your inheritance money at a private health clinic which will perform liposuction on your most unsightly fatty deposits, when the alternative is to own up to your lack of motivation to embark on regular outdoor activities.

It is surprisingly easy for some experts to reel you in with pseudoscience and mystifying words or formulas, and sway you to invest a sizeable amount of hard-earned income into acquiring their exclusive product. Such products claim to change your life for the better, whilst allowing you to continue with your comfortable sub-optimal diet and stressful lifestyle. According to the Dulwich Health website their unique product, OxyTech™ (a specially formulated Magnesium Oxide compound with Activated Oxygen enhancement along with Vitamin C and Bioflavoid(*sic*) Complex), can clear up candidiasis in two to three weeks. Data supporting these claims are not listed on the webpage.

Be sure not to confuse OxyTech™ with the more popular, now discontinued, Milk of Magnesium or indeed with Epsom salts. These three products share the same basic compound (magnesium). However, the latter two have frequently been used as a laxative in the past; Milk of Magnesium was a common household treatment for constipation.

Instant fixes and unbelievable claims pave the way for unrealistic expectations. They also help support an industry that has branded everything from infant formula to meal-replacement beverages as 'real food'.

During the 1980s fitness gurus and health experts advocated the indiscriminate limitation of all fats in the diet, which set in motion the 'anti-fat revolution'. The disconcerting after-effect is that the incidence of obesity has increased on a global scale, from childhood to adulthood, particularly in societies where the Western or standard American/British diet has been adopted. Butter was substituted with margarine because of cholesterol fears; today, we are bombarded by messages stating that the range of Benecol® products can reduce cholesterol by 7–10% in just 3 weeks. Given that this product contains plant material (plant stanol ester), why can we not suggest that patients at risk of high cholesterol eat plant-based foods? For many people, using mashed up avocado instead of butter (or indeed, any other kind of spread) on their morning toast or lunchtime sandwich is a simple, realistic, and maintainable strategy, with very possibly a better health outcome, and ultimately, a more enjoyable eating experience.

The path to my clinic door has visible marks of footfall due to the hundreds of patients, ranging from the very famous to the girl next door. They seek me out to help them improve their health. People who are physically incapacitated, restricted, or just rendered miserable by their dietary choices, all too often following diets they think are 'healthy'. Some people need help avoiding frequent recurring colds, women often need guidance in correcting female hormone imbalances, and countless requests are to address gut related symptoms, from irritable bowel syndrome to inflammatory bowel disease. Tears of desperation flow often in my clinic room, because patients are finally allowed to share their story, from the beginning up to where they are now, and because they know that help is finally at hand. The countless letters of gratitude and subsequent tales of unexpected health improvement are the ultimate accolade in my vocation. Many letters reach me years after my last contact with an individual and reflect on how easy it is to still follow my recommendations. That is all because my simple health strategy, which I will outline in detail in this book, is realistic, congruent with the patient's lifestyle, and ultimately maintainable long-term. This successful blueprint focuses on food, real, appetising, nutritious food. To quote Oscar Wilde, I hate people who are not serious about meals. It is so shallow of them.

# Introduction

The field of human nutrition is evolving, and emerging scientific findings are only selectively published in the popular media. This results in an overly passionate discussion, making this exciting field of health research appear more like a battleground. Finger pointing, insults, and public ridicule are being dished out left right and centre, in print and on social media. Food is an emotive subject, and tempers run high when ideologies are challenged. The most vocal in this ongoing public battle are popular personalities speaking out against modern-day bloggers; these bloggers publish the most appetising food photographs on a daily basis and are accused of creating a cultish following at the risk of long-term health issues for their followers. Behind the scenes are highly qualified scientists who quietly review the latest scientific literature, work with food, and run successful patient clinics. As one camp raises its profile, the opposition becomes more vocal. Angry responses and the derision of passionate individuals dominate social media, individuals who sadly do not hold formal nutritional, or even scientific, educational qualifications.

In the middle of all of this is a population which is becoming more distrustful of the experts and their ever-changing views, overwhelmed with the demands of the modern day, plagued with illness, and desperately searching symptom relief – most people do not have time to sift through all the arguments and scientific jargon. Why are our food choices rife with such inconsistencies and factional malice?

# What Insight Is Revealed in Clinical Practice?

In my clinic, I see many people at the end of their tether, suffering from conditions that have so far not been successfully addressed by either conventional medicine or complementary, alternative therapies. The majority of the work I do focuses on digestive tract disorders, conditions like Irritable Bowel Syndrome (IBS), Inflammatory Bowel Disease (IBD), and female hormonal health, including Pre-Menstrual Syndrome (PMS) and menopause. Investigating and addressing the underlying causes of the symptoms presented requires an in-depth understanding of a patient's health, medical history, lifestyle choices, and the biological status quo. A completed comprehensive questionnaire and food diary help me prepare for an in-depth, one-to-one consultation. Laboratory tests may be needed as one part of the understanding of what lies at the root of each patient's presenting symptoms. Once extensive information has been gathered, a protocol is tailored to each patient's needs and their stated health goals, enabling them to embark on the road to recovery. Each patient I see is unique; their needs are unlikely to be met by reading any one book or any amount of googling. Addressing health concerns often requires expert assistance, and often involves more than one expert. However, in my years of clinical experience, I have found one thing that is invariably overwhelmingly beneficial; improving their diet.

## The Aim of This Book

This book focuses on food choices; in particular, the minimum dietary requirements needed to support health, and the optimal diet to promote the best health outcome. My simple health strategy introduces you to the main basic components of healthy human nutrition. This realistic strategy is for everyone, young and old, and to incorporate these changes into your daily life you do not need to be an elite athlete at the very apex of your career, or indeed have world-class cooking skills. There is no need for a calibrated scale, paid membership, a downloadable app, or indeed a technical handbook to follow this simple health strategy. The only tool you need is this book, which will show you how powerful dietary changes normally are, and how you can help yourself to be the best that you can be.

This strategy can be maintained long-term. It introduces three components that should be present at all meals; these will ensure that you are supported, at least to a base level, with regards to macronutrients, and essential vitamins and minerals which promote optimal health. The three pillars are vegetables, protein, and carbohydrates. To optimise your health, the key is to prioritise these three pillars in the order listed: vegetables take prime importance, followed by the other two macronutrients listed, protein and carbohydrates.

This is exactly what food manufacturers do. When you look at the ingredient list printed on packaged food you will see a series of components that indicate the most abundant ones first, and the least abundant ones last. For example, if we look at the very popular breakfast cereal, Kellogg's® Corn Flakes, the first ingredient is corn (89%), followed by sugar, salt, barley, malt extract, vitamins and minerals. Clearly, corn is the main ingredient; the vitamins and minerals are present in quantities far less than that of corn. Have a look at the different ingredients next time you need to decide between two similar products and remember that the first ingredient is the main component. This works for any type of product, oven fries, yoghurt, even beer.

My simple, realistic, and maintainable health strategy states that the most abundant ingredient of all your meals should be vegetables, then protein and lastly carbohydrates (also termed 'starch'). This book will show that the ideal plate composition consists of ½ **V**egetables, ¼ **P**rotein, and ¼ **C**arbohydrates. No matter how big or small your chosen plate, the aim is to ensure that you fill half of it with an array of non-starchy vegetables, include one-quarter of protein dense food, and ensure that there are no more carbohydrates or starch than protein on your plate. Just so that we are clear on what non-starch vegetables are, they tend to be the ones which are vibrant green, red, or yellow. Starchy vegetables (carbohydrates), on the other hand, are more often white, pale yellow, brown, or similar colours; for example, potatoes, rutabaga (Swedish turnip), turnips, sweet potato, yam, winter squashes, and peas (even though they are obviously green). These starchy vegetables are also packed with a host of nutrients, but should not be your only choices at meal times.

Whether you are a growing child, a doting grandparent, proud homemaker, powerful businessman, or internationally recognised musician, you are probably someone who would like to optimise your health. We all know that there is no magic pill or fail-safe shortcut to better health. Now that you have taken the first step of finding out how to be in the best possible health, the next step is to become completely engaged in the process. It is without a doubt that the best patient outcomes are achieved when a person actively takes part in the whole process, from seeking out the relevant specialist, to following and implementing the much-sought expert advice. Joining a gym make you fit, but only once you regularly attend classes or complete the weight training circuit. Similarly, nutritious meals only come as the result of you taking the time to shop, choose the right ingredients, prepare a delicious dinner, and, ultimately, enjoy every bite. Nutrition is *the* primary therapy for optimising your health goals, not an alternative therapy. Without eating, we die, and by eating incorrectly we drastically limit how healthy we can be. The key is to try to make the best choices, every day, for the rest of your life.

## The Link Between Nutrition and Ill Health

Since nutrition (or more appropriately, malnutrition) is so often at the heart of chronic health problems, we shall start by looking at the various ways in which changing your diet can help to tackle and overcome symptoms associated with conditions such as fatigue, IBS, eczema, stress, PMS, and even IBD. This journey into the world of optimum nutrition will help you change your life.

The problems and challenges faced by most people, be it you or someone dear to you, usually fall into one of a select few areas. Probably the most frequent struggle I encounter, and one which we will address in detail is the battle with what we could call 'lifestyle' factors like fatigue and stress. These conditions can be the result of a frenetic lifestyle, work or home pressures, like raising a family or looking after someone who is unwell or even just trying to keep up with this busy world that we live in.

So many people are juggling work and home lives, perhaps studying full or part-time or planning on changing careers; whatever the reason, being stressed and feeling tired all the time is a huge burden to carry. An environment where coffee, alcohol, rich food, smoking, and perhaps even recreational drugs dominate will not rectify the situation. But sadly, not everybody who is stressed can realistically change their work hours, let alone get away from it all by jetting off to an island or a health retreat, even though often either would certainly help. What you can do is change your diet.

For women, hormonal health can be a big issue starting in adolescence and continuing well beyond the menopause. That timespan can stretch over a staggering four decades. The concerns can include depression, anxiety, mood swings, irregular menses, heavy bleeding, debilitating cramps, skin conditions such as distressing acne, hot flushes, and – although rarely spoken about – low libido. Fatigue, associated with hormonal imbalances, is a major concern because it can have such a huge impact on a woman's life both associated with work and enjoying a healthy social life. Hormonal fluctuations are normal; but when a woman experiences symptoms that impact her day-to-day life, it is time to investigate underlying causes. Food plays a major role because for a few days every month, sweet cravings seem to dominate. I cannot count how many times I have heard women tell me that they follow two diets, one for a week a month and another, vastly different one the rest of the time. Arranging food choices to conform to the ideal plate composition is necessary to prevent such cravings from ruling erratic eating behaviour fuelled by hormonal imbalances.

A further complication of being a woman is the change in thyroid hormones that control our metabolic rates. When a woman reaches her 40's it is not uncommon for the thyroid gland to stop functioning optimally. Its compromised hormone production negatively impacts on your ability to lose weight, on bowel movement regularity, on joint health, and on energy levels. It is no wonder that fatigue is such an important lifestyle factor given that it is so easily affected by hormones, nutritional status, sleep habits, and pace of life. A lifetime of eating habits irrefutably impacts vitality and, even though you may not be able to maintain a steady level of vibrancy in your later years, there is no reason why you cannot remain active throughout your life. Good food choices in line with this book's health strategy enables you to enjoy life – no matter how many grey hairs have made their appearance.

At the other end of the age range, we see an increasing number of infants and young children affected by the skin condition, eczema (atopic dermatitis). Areas of the face, arms, or legs may be affected, or you might have a child who is covered from the top of the head to the tip of the toes in an angry red rash. This distressing skin condition is the result of poor gut health and unsuitable food choices; as a result, affected individuals need to be very vigilant when choosing food or beverages. Stress is another very important contributing factor and many adults who suffer find themselves stress eating. This clearly exacerbates, rather than alleviates, *any* skin condition (be it eczema, acne, or psoriasis). Nutrient-dense vegetables are not top of any binge eating food list. That list is almost exclusively reserved for snacks (savoury or sweet), alcohol, and coffee or other energy drinks. There are, of course, many creams available on the market that alleviate skin conditions, but, just like in the case of fatigue and hormonal imbalances, the biggest impact is made by the food you put on your plate.

Probably the most common complaint I encounter is IBS; even when it is not the main issue, many patients mention that their bowel misbehaves at times, often following some form of stress, foreign travel, or medication. A diet rich in refined carbohydrates can wreak havoc with most healthy guts, and when we find ourselves in an environment rife with junk food, alcohol, and quick energy snacks, IBS symptoms can make an unwelcome appearance. For both IBS and IBD sufferers, choosing these readily available options can additionally result in unwanted weight issues, which is often an issue raised in a clinical setting. For IBD patients who have been diagnosed with incurable Crohn's disease, incorrect food choices can have catastrophic consequences.

## The Elephant in the Room, Weight Concerns

When we talk about excess weight, it is important to note that meals largely based on refined carbohydrates are detrimental to healthy weight goals. You may have heard that obesity is largely related to our genes, and only minimally associated with the sheer quantity of processed food on the market and negative lifestyle choices. However, it is very difficult to find a serious argument against the importance of minimising starch options in our diets. Adopting a high protein, high saturated fat diet is not the answer either. As a matter of fact, it is likely to cause more harm than good in the long-term, just like any other fad (or 'exclusive') diet that is making the rounds and promising unrealistic outcomes. Substituting food with meal-replacement drinks, focusing on one superfood, chewing your food a minimum of 40 times: these are all short-lived endeavours. Putting all your faith in a fat burning pill is verging on dangerous territory, despite the numerous clinical trials quoted in support of these prescriptive options. Eating real food in the way that is conducive to good health is the only way to successfully stabilise your weight in line with your genetic make-up and activity levels.

The answer to excess weight or obesity is complex; mere calorie restriction has repeatedly been shown to fall short of permanent success. Any successful weight loss programme includes nutrient-dense food selection, regular exercise, and psychological support to facilitate changes in those habits which drive mindless and excess eating. Eating disorder clinics, who mainly deal with underweight patients, always include talk therapy as one of the main pillars of treatment. Yet, when we encounter overweight patients, the instant response is, 'just stop eating so much' or 'put the doughnut down'. The struggle for obese patients having to adjust their diet and lifestyle to lose weight is every bit as real as the difficulty anorexic patients have willingly consuming regular, nutrient-dense meals.

There are vanishingly few individuals who can eat what they want in any quantity throughout their lives without any detrimental weight fluctuations. These people are extreme exceptions, not the rule. People who are born into overweight families are able to change their body composition by omitting non-essential food and remaining active throughout their lives: these are conscious and lifelong endeavours. Some people are naturally slim and ill-advised food choices or inactivity may not express in visible excess weight. However, if your genetic makeup predisposes you to easy weight gain, your health strategy will need to involve careful food choices, frequent physical activity, and awareness of the pitfalls of dietary and lifestyle vices for the rest of your life. To believe that your dietary choices and lifestyle factors will not affect your genetic expression is short-sighted. Arya Sharma, M.D. PhD., states that even though diet and exercise remain a cornerstone for treatment, they simply are not effective enough to control obesity in most people who have it. He advocates that we classify obesity as a disease and channel treatment options which are used for cancer, diabetes, and heart disease care as part of addressing this growing problem. All this highlights the complexity of weight management and the realisation that, even though dietary choices are fundamental, obese patients may not realise their weight goals without additional lifestyle changes, psychological support and medical intervention, which might include surgery. In my clinic weight loss, and weight gain where required, are a consequence of improved health, not a goal.

## The Ideal Plate Strategy

My rules are simple and powerful and may strike you as contradictory to the traditional food pyramid and NHS Eatwell Guide, which strongly promote carbohydrates as the bulk of meals and protein only forming a small fraction. Those two major eating guides continue to insist that dairy options should *always* be included despite the extensive scientific material and populations studies that do not support this dogma. This book neither focuses on nor considers, calorie restriction as a sensible approach for weight loss; this is not just another low carbohydrate diet, advising avoidance of all root vegetables and legumes. Vegetables, in all varieties, shapes, and sizes bring key nutrients to the table. This is particularly important when science shows us how important non-starch vegetables are in terms of gut health, and the indispensable role protein has to play in genetic material, cell replication, hormone secretion, muscle formation, and growth and repair processes, to name but a few areas. Starches or carbohydrates are an excellent source of energy, and choosing nutrient-dense options ensures that you fulfil your nutritional needs. Think of their inclusion as completing the circle.

To successfully address your nutritional needs, fatigue, stress response, gut health, weight concerns, hormonal imbalances, and skin health, you need to look at the food on your plate and compare it with the ideal plate, consisting of ½ **V**egetables, ¼ **P**rotein, and ¼ **C**arbohydrates. You do not need a newly invented food pyramid, a 10-step programme, a 15-minute workout, that elusive super-berry now being mass produced at the other end of the globe, or possibly sometimes even anti-depressant medication. You simply need to reorganise the foods you reach for, at home and eating out, to be in line with the ideal plate composition, no matter the size of your chosen plate. These rules are supported in the latest health research and open the door to enjoying food, real food, the kind of food that does not line a board of directors' pockets. The kind of food our farmers are putting their heart and soul into producing without destroying the rainforests or protected land. The kind of food that nature gives us in abundance, irrespective of the seasons. The kind of food that collects nutrients from the soil, the air, and water, which is imperative in enabling our biology to function optimally. The kind of food that has allowed us to populate the Earth, generation after generation.

Science is not a democracy and sometimes it tells us what we do not want to hear or, indeed, to apply to our lives. The collected data irrefutably shows that diets high in plant fibre, inclusive of protein-rich options, and nutrient-dense carbohydrates are conducive to positive health outcomes. Diets low in vegetables and essential nutrients lead to serious conditions, sub-optimal body weight, and even long-term diseases. We all need an optimal diet to enable us to live life to the full and minimise our risk of developing diseases; when a person already has a diagnosed condition, then this dietary focus is even more important. The choice is ultimately yours to make. Set your health goals, be realistic in your aims, stay committed, and choose to be the best that you can be. Now dear reader, let your journey to healthy eating begin.

# Prepare Your Plate for Optimum Function

## Heather's Story

In May 2010 Heather, a 45-year-old doting grandmother, came to the clinic seeking help with suspected food intolerances, ongoing fatigue, and excess weight. She was not diagnosed with one particular condition but rather needed guidance with regards to her current diet.

*****

Heather has striking, bright blue eyes and her short brown hair is beautifully styled. There is a deep dimple on her right cheek and she effortlessly engages in conversation. She has travelled all the way from Cowbridge in Wales, which in itself is no small feat given that she suffers from ongoing chronic fatigue.

"Wilma, you need to help me. I have to choose between work and living, I simply cannot do both."

This is a desperate cry for help and makes one realise how much is at stake. It is not unusual for people to utter heart-wrenching pleas for help such as 'you are my last hope' when they are at the end of their tether. When a patient has been suffering for years and has seen many experts during that time, there inevitably comes a point where they feel that the whole journey must end somewhere. As many health experts can attest, there appears to be a myriad of people who are walking around suffering from one illness or another. Illnesses that range from frequent headaches to cancer and even though some people suffer in silence, others wear their illnesses like an integral part of their identity. Only when a patient finds a viable plan of action can the healing begin and a process of redefinition of identity ensues. Heather did not want to be called Heather, the one without energy.

Heather's diet was overwhelmingly focused on carbohydrates and starch options and noticeably low on vegetables. I suspect that the weather in Cowbridge is not comparable to a more Mediterranean climate and given that it is a small town with less than 5000 inhabitants, the availability of a variety of fresh vegetables is different to that of the capital, Cardiff. When the average temperature seldom rises above 20°C, and that is in summer, the prospect of eating a hearty salad made with an assortment of fresh, raw vegetables is not everyone's cup of tea. The preferred choice of food, as in Heather's case, is hot, starchy-carbohydrate heavy meals which provide both heat in this colder climate, and is ultimately perceived as more satisfying. Many households decide on what carbohydrate option will be the centre point of each meal before deciding on any other accompaniments. Given that the traditional food pyramid and NHS Eatwell Guide strongly promote carbohydrates as the bulk of all meals, the rationale behind this method of planning dinner is quite easy to understand.

Heather is a mere 152 cm (5 foot) tall and her weight is 68 kg (10 stone 10), meaning that she is classified as overweight and, according to her body mass index (BMI) reading of 29, on the verge of obesity. It is rather a common occurrence for women over the age of 40 to stand on the bathroom scales and wonder where it all went wrong. Getting onto those scales is an emotional rollercoaster ride at the best of times but when you look at the numbers and know in your heart that you are doing all that you possibly can and the results are just not in your favour, frustration and unhappiness are regular bedfellows. It transpired that Heather, like many young people who aspire to an ideal weight, followed extreme diets during her 20s. Fad diets, which promote the exclusion of a food or indeed a food group can significantly impact on your health. These diets can result in rapid weight loss but once you stop dieting, you find yourself piling on those lost pounds again. Robert Dilts calls these yo-yo diets, "The rhythm method of girth control."

Extreme exclusion diets such as the cabbage soup diet, the master cleanse diet, the grapefruit diet, the Hallelujah diet, the tapeworm diet, and even the blood-type diet, to name but a few, all advocate cutting a food or sometimes a whole food group from your daily diet. All this to reach an unrealistic weight goal in a short space of time.

## What Are Short-Term and Extreme Diets?

Let us take some time to look at the types of extreme diets that, I am sure, most of you will have considered or even tried at one time or another. First the infamous cabbage soup diet, which on the surface, sounds like a good investment given that it is based around a vegetable, cabbage. Cabbage is but one vegetable in a list of many and by only eating warm cabbage you forfeit other crucial macronutrients, like protein and carbohydrates, and essential micronutrients in the form of vital vitamins and minerals. Even one meal on this diet robs you of key nutrients, never mind following this extreme regime for an extended period of time. Similarly, the master cleanse diet advocates the intake of lemon water flavoured with maple syrup and cayenne pepper. Apart from lemon, this extreme diet is completely void of all the essential food groups. The grapefruit diet combines a high protein, high-fat diet, similar to the Atkins diet, with grapefruit, because it professes grapefruit's ability to burn fat. Here we have a diet that includes protein and fat, albeit the unhealthy saturated options, but like those previously mentioned, is void of nutritious vegetable options. On the flip-side of this particular gem we meet the Hallelujah diet which encourages dieters to eat a diet believed to have been followed by Adam and Eve in the garden of Eden, thus fruit, vegetables, and whole grains. As a diet, it is starting to include valuable plant matter but still falls short of an all-inclusive health strategy. The raw food diet similarly opens your world to the wonders of fruit, vegetables, nuts, and seeds but it too continues to exclude necessary nutrients.

Extreme and short-term diets have one goal in mind and that is weight reduction. From the high-protein, high-fat Atkins diet to the calorie restrictive Weight Watchers Smart Points option, the aim is to enable a person to shed unwanted weight without considering long-term nutritional status or health outcome. Our overwhelming desire to conform to an unrealistic weight at all cost is putting our health in danger. No sacrifice is deemed too large as long as the weight benefits are realised within the shortest time possible. If results take more than a month to be noticed, then people will simply move on to the latest wonder diet, frequently endorsed by a much-admired celebrity, sporting an enviable figure. Similarly, many people gravitate towards a vegetarian or vegan diet with the sole purpose of losing weight. We see countless adolescents who are slim and even dangerously underweight who develop serious nutrient deficiencies. Deficiencies that impact a normal day to day function of our biology including growth and development. When we look at girls aged between 11 and 18 who restrict their diets either by minimising calories or by excluding certain food groups, we see a large group of people who are at high risk of developing anaemia. The high cost of iron-deficiency anaemia is an altered or suppressed menstrual cycle, making it difficult to conceive later on in life. Being thin is clearly not the ultimate yardstick for good health.

The biological stress that yo-yo dieting and extreme diets have on your physiology can lead to many health complications where the most frequently noted is micronutrient deficiencies. Humans derive crucial vitamins and minerals from food and when we avoid or severely restrict the intake thereof, purely because we are focused on weight reduction, we risk developing diseases in later years. This is a dear price to pay just to look good in an outfit or indeed on the beach that one two-week holiday abroad a year.

Back to Heather. Her yo-yo dieting caused her weight to plummet to 44.5 kg (7 stone) and a serious health scare at 25 resulted in Heather undergoing surgery to remove a large part of her thyroid gland. The thyroid gland controls our metabolism and when the thyroid hormones are affected it is not uncommon to experience undesired weight issues post-intervention. If you are a woman over 40 you should consider having your thyroid function tested if you have not done so already, particularly if the following symptoms apply to you:

- Lethargy, fatigue or poor stamina,
- Constipation,
- Sensitivity to cold temperatures in the hands and feet,
- Coarse hair or hair loss,
- Dry skin, particularly the heels of the feet,
- Inability to shed unwanted weight,
- High blood cholesterol levels,
- Joint pains which can be associated with swelling or stiffness,
- Increase in menstrual flow and even irregular menstrual cycles,
- Low mood or depression,
- Muscle weakness.

Despite Heather focusing on achieving her ideal weight during her twenties, the end result was that, 20 years later, her weight was far from her original goal. The amount of excess weight that she was carrying can put a noticeable strain on joints, especially the knees, the spinal cord, and eventually impede one's day to day physical activity.

## Getting the Full Health Picture

In order to understand a patient's health journey, information starting from birth to the present date needs to be gathered. How long someone has been suffering from their presenting symptoms is as important to establish as any dietary changes. For example, if someone presents with an impeccable daily diet you need to establish how long that person has been eating this way. If you have changed your diet recently it may take your body a while longer to benefit from this new regime. Unlike an electrical socket, your body does not have only two functions, on or off. Your physiology is incredibly complex and even the experts are aware that we understand but a fraction of the inner workings of the human biology. To expect instant changes after the introduction of one nutritious meal, or even a week's worth is unrealistic. The old adage of 'slow and steady wins the race' is the mantra we should adopt when it comes to nutrition.

Heather's life story revealed that she was diagnosed with depression when she was only 15 and was also treated for Stevens-Johnson Syndrome, a rare and serious condition which is often linked to a severe reaction to medication. Her father and a dear friend passed away when she was 40 and as a result, her consultant prescribed anti-depressant medication. Her doctor additionally prescribed an iron supplement given that she was complaining about low energy and subsequent blood tests confirmed that she was indeed anaemic. Heather says that she is reliant on the iron supplement because without it she really has no energy at all. Here is a lady of 45 who has been on thyroid medication for approximately 20 years, an iron supplement, anti-depressants, and medication to reduce the acid in her stomach because, in addition to all her other complaints, she also experienced stomach pain.

Do any of Heather's complaints sound familiar? If so, take a moment to write down your own health history to see just how long you have been suffering from a particular symptom and also how long you have been taking certain medications. Do include over the counter headache tablets, antacids, anti-inflammatory pills, and even the oral contraceptive pill. Remember to include any diets that you might have tried as well. And if you have ever suffered from an eating disorder, such as anorexia or bulimia, never neglect to mention this to your healthcare professional.

Before we go further, let us look at Heather's plate composition so that we can see what she was eating. Looking at Heather's plate we can immediately see how it is dominated by carbohydrates at the expense of much-needed protein and fundamental vegetable options.

### Heather's Plate Composition

The ideal plate composition, in contrast, should consist of ½ **V**egetables, ¼ **P**rotein, and ¼ **C**arbohydrates.

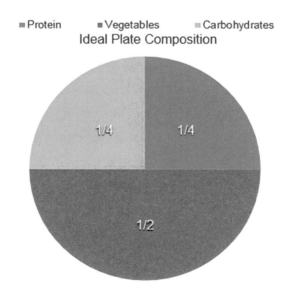

Heather experienced a host of digestive complaints and, like many others, she started wondering if some of her food choices were indeed beneficial to her current gut function or if she should embark on an elimination diet to identify possible food culprits. We know that the gold standard test for food sensitivities is an elimination (oligoantigenic) diet and that process can be laborious and can extend over weeks or even months before results are amassed. Patients run the risk of avoiding many essential food options because, after much trial and error, they are left with a meagre handful of options. This was indeed the case with Heather because her self-motivated in-depth investigation showed that options such as soya, fruit, most vegetables, wine, and the commonly used flavour enhancer, monosodium glutamate (MSG) seemed to exacerbate her presenting symptoms. There are indeed a handful of food options that seem to affect digestive function in a large percentage of people and those include soya, eggs, corn, some nuts and seeds, wheat, and bovine dairy. Note that vegetables, except for corn, do not form part of that list of commonly encountered obvious culprits. Heather identified one of those common problem foods, soya, but what raised concerns was that she felt that most vegetables were also problematic. And strangely enough, corn was not even on her list. Given that years of blood testing at the clinic has shown that vegetables are the least allergenic foods, it was time to show Heather how the results of her self-investigation were flawed.

## Why Are Vegetables so Important?

While you consider your own plate composition, let us explore what vegetables actually bring to the table, so to speak. The most discussed benefit is fibre, which is associated with good bowel movements, so in essence a treatment option for constipation. Given that there are many breakfast cereals that are high in fibre does it mean that we do not need to include vegetables and fruit when a traditional Western breakfast option can take care of our daily fibre needs? In fact, there used to be health clinics that specialised in treating constipated patients with cereal-based fibre. First of all, plant material, in the form of vegetables and fruit, have been part of our dietary makeup much longer than grains, the main ingredient of breakfast cereals. This means that your body has expertly adapted to extract essential nutrients from vegetables and fruit, whereas the adaptation to eating a diet predominantly focused on cereal grains is still proving problematic for many people. Our evolution is not yet complete. Your ancestors' ancestors might have maintained perfect health on a diet rich in cereal, but you, the one with the gut issues, might be sensitive to this type of fibre. Secondly, unlike grains which are fortified, vegetables naturally contain a host of important vitamins and minerals which contribute towards making your unique body function optimally. The increasing rise of food allergies and coeliac disease furthermore make consumption of most dietary grains, such as gluten-containing options, unsuitable for an increasing number of people. Remember that one of the more common problematic food ingredients for a large percentage of people is wheat, a gluten-containing grain, which is the main ingredient of most bread, pasta, and baked goods, the very ingredients strongly promoted by the traditional food pyramid and Eatwell Plate.

Arguably the most important benefit of ensuring that your meals contain ½ a plate of vegetables is their role in promoting the growth and diversity of the trillions of beneficial bacteria in the gut. Even though food first enters the mouth, moves down the oesophagus, and enters the stomach (the only notably acidic part of your anatomy), it takes some time to eventually get to the epicentre of digestion, the small bowel or commonly referred to as the gut. Here, digestive enzymes work their magic in breaking down food into small particles and releasing important vitamins and minerals needed for your biology to function optimally. This microcosm of bacteria present in vast quantities in the gut ultimately determine your health status. Their role in health is complex and diverse and despite extensive research, their full function is still not completely understood. Beneficial bacteria thrive when you eat a variety of vegetables and fruit and as their numbers increase they prevent the growth of bad bacteria, parasites, and unwanted yeast in the gut, the three components that contribute to ill-health. Pre-biotic vegetable fibre essentially creates an environment in which the good bacteria can prosper.

**Table 1**. Vegetables to boost good gut bacteria
Raw chicory root
Jerusalem artichoke
Dandelion greens
Garlic
Leeks
Onions

You are most certainly familiar with the term probiotic, of which yoghurt is considered a good source. Probiotics contain strains of the actual beneficial bacteria that should be found in the human gut. However, given the environment in which these strains of bacteria live, a vast proportion of them cannot be cultured in a laboratory. These bacteria can only survive in an environment where oxygen is absent and given that all life on Earth exposed to air require oxygen to survive, it is difficult to find an environment where oxygen is not present, even in very small quantities. Even though we can cultivate strains like *lactobacillus acidophilus* in commercial yoghurt we are completely incapable of cultivating many of the other strains of good bacteria found in the human gut. Eating ½ a plate of vegetables ensures that you regularly eat foods that are able to feed those good bacteria already present in your gut. The added advantage is that you are not spending money on products whose efficacy has been under scrutiny of late.

## Vegetable Intake and Health Conditions

Apart from digestive irregularities, such as constipation, other gut conditions are also associated with lack of vegetable intake in the diet, which include bacterial infections, IBS, and IBD. But it is not only our gut health that benefits from eating vegetables, the likelihood of you developing a host of other debilitating diseases can be minimised simply by adopting this simple health strategy. Arguably the most important organ in our bodies, the heart, also benefits greatly from changing your plate composition to include ½ a plate of vegetables. Lowered blood pressure and cholesterol, traditional health markers associated with heart health, are irrefutably linked with the intake of vegetables. The various global heart foundations are very vocal in advocating a diet which includes plenty of fruit and vegetables to minimise the risk of cardiovascular disease and stroke. Similarly, the National Eye Institute (NEI) recommends eating a healthy diet rich in leafy green vegetables to significantly reduce your risk of developing the common eye condition, Age-related Macular Degeneration (AMD). This debilitating condition affects people aged 50 years and over and can lead to loss of vision. At the other end of the health spectrum, lack of vegetable fibre is linked with one of the most commonly occurring forms of cancer, colon cancer.

You can see that there are many conditions that respond positively to the inclusion of an abundance of vegetables in the diet and even though medical advances now allow us to treat most of these diseases successfully without any dietary or lifestyle changes, the long-term outcome is undoubtedly supported with the inclusion of a nutrient-dense diet. You can roll the dice and take your chances but a person might prefer to prevent an illness rather than hope for a cure.

## The Role of Your Good Gut Bacteria

There is overwhelming data to support a diet consisting of mainly plant material as the best diet for humans. Emerging evidence shows that a predominantly plant-based diet contributes to a wider range of beneficial (friendly) gut bacteria, which is associated with improved health outcomes. Tim Spector, professor of genetic epidemiology, and his team of researchers at King's College London are compiling a comprehensive human gut microbiome database to show the vast variation as it relates to each individual's geographical location, genetic makeup, and diet. Their research is sure to pave the way for other experts in the field to present their findings on this topic of increasing interest. By collating all the relevant data in the future, we can be sure to gain insight into the correlation between certain illnesses and specific gut bacteria.

## Health Agency Guidelines

Guidelines state that each person should be including five portions of vegetables and fruit in their daily diet. When we compare this message to emerging data and the World Health

Organisation (WHO) recommendations, we see that 5-a-day is the bare minimum and barely scratches the surface when addressing long-term health outcomes. We know that most families in the UK do not consume 5-a-day, and in fact, there are too many households where vegetables and fruit are completely absent. The NHS reports that a mere 26% of the UK population regularly eat 5-a-day, that translates to 1 in 4 people. Heather's household was no exception.

Next time you shop, have a look at your fellow shoppers and see what they have chosen to put in their baskets. Chances are a small fraction of the average basket or trolley contains any produce gathered in the vegetable aisle, but a large percentage will contain a bag of potatoes or ready cut French fries. The research highlighting the health benefits of plant-based food other than the starch options is overwhelming and yet it appears that the message is not powerful enough to motivate the majority of the population to challenge their taste buds. We can attribute this attitude to many different factors, ranging from low household income, lack of available fresh produce, and time constraints. In my experience, the biggest reason for avoiding vegetables is personal choice related to bad eating habits.

The challenge is to accept that you cannot refute the science supporting the health benefits of a diet which includes vegetables and fruit. Once you have made peace with the fact that you have to change your point of view and learn to enjoy vegetables, the next step is to include a wide variety of vegetable options at all meals to entice everybody around the dinner table to sample and hopefully, discover a viable option, or indeed, five. If we only ever present one or two of the same vegetable options at mealtimes it is no surprise that too many people, especially children, dislike an extensive list of these important food choices. We furthermore need to be mindful of our language around food. It is not uncommon to hear people refer to vegetable as those yucky options. If the language we use to describe nutrient-dense food is this negative and conversely overwhelmingly positive in its use when talking about non-essential options (special treat, sweets, naughty indulgence), then it is no small wonder that the majority of consumers flock towards the dessert, biscuit, and soft drinks aisles in preference to the fresh produce section or the local farmer's market.

Even though a lot of people have developed a taste for fruit it is not surprising that many people do not like vegetables, given the quality of produce that is commonly on sale. The agricultural objective is firstly to fulfil quotas as set by the purchaser and then to grow produce that conforms to a certain aesthetically pleasing standard. Consumers tend to avoid buying ugly and irregular shaped produce in favour of the shiniest, biggest, more perfectly symmetrical offerings, which often lack flavour.

Nutrition experts can have a myopic view when it comes to food by focusing on the nutrient content and health benefits of eating. There is another class of person who specialises in food who has a very different view, chefs, especially those who cook to the highest culinary standards. One of these experts is an internationally acclaimed chef, Dan Barber, who owns and cooks at Blue Hill at Stone Barns in New York, who is very vocal about the importance of growing produce which tantalises the taste buds. He works directly with local farmers to create crops that are both ethically sourced and sustainable, but most importantly, bursting with flavour. His unconventional, ground-breaking approach to meal ingredients showcases world-renowned dishes that are changing the course of traditional dining. We are finally moving in a direction where people are starting to demand tasty food and thus looking beyond ornate table settings and intricate decor at the expense of a memorable gastronomic experience.

## Making Vegetables the Nation's First Choice

The key to enticing people to choose to buy vegetables is to make produce available that results in a taste experience comparable or ideally better than non-nutritious food options which are marketed for their intense flavour. People tend to snack on flavoured crisps or a bag of intensely sweet candy instead of a plate of crudités. The reason is that, unlike raw vegetables, the preferred snack options tend to contain strong flavours, which allow you to satisfy a craving. How often have you looked at a salad and immediately decided that you would not enjoy it unless a strong-flavoured salad dressing was added in copious amounts?  Some people only enjoy vegetables if it is complemented with a cheese sauce, gravy, or generous helping of vinegar.  Three-star Michelin Chef Enrico Crippa's signature dish, Insalata 21, 31, 41, 51, contains a combination of up to 51 different lettuce and herbs (depending on availability) served without a dressing and is lauded as one of the tastiest options on the exquisite seasonal menu.  When you eat at his restaurant in Alba, Italy, you are almost certain to dine on a meal that contains 70% vegetables.  This phenomenal amount of fresh produce is freshly gathered every morning from his two and a half hectare garden tended by four full-time staff.  Enrico shows that you do not have to sacrifice flavour when aiming for nutritious content.

Yes, people who actually like an array of vegetables may have a more sensitive palate, but the overwhelming drive behind avoiding vegetables is that we have become embroiled in questionable habits.  If you desire a better health outcome then it is time to re-educate your palate, break the trend and nurture new healthy behaviour.  Ultimately, making sense of human nutrition can be perplexing and by reading this important book you can learn to identify the different nutrients, their role in health, and translate this knowledge into practical application in your daily life.  Nobody is too young or too old to adopt optimal food choices.

## What Happened to Heather?

My contact with Heather spanned three years and in that time, we introduced different food options yielding excellent results with weight loss as an added bonus.  By introducing ½ a plate of vegetables and reducing her carbohydrate and starch options to ¼ of her plate, Heather not only continued to supply her body with adequate amounts of energy, she more importantly added necessary vitamins and minerals obtained from her newly chosen vegetable options.  The ideal plate composition does not advocate the avoidance of carbohydrate-rich foods, but rather successfully shows that unless you are an elite athlete you simply do not need more than ¼ of a plate because your energy needs are not high enough to warrant such a bountiful intake.

Heather's diet severely lacked a variety of vegetables, which was rectified by showing her that there was a vast array of delicious options which she could source locally, purchase without breaking the bank, prepare without fuss, and ultimately enjoy along with her family. We walked her path to improved health together and made sure that we discussed the importance of inclusive food choices because too many patients are focused on avoiding what they perceive, often without sound confirmation, as being the obvious food culprits. When it comes to nutrition, what you put on your plate is as important as what you avoid. Optimum food choices are not about food avoidance, it is about adding vital nutrients in the form of real food. The ultimate aim is not to lose weight, it is about gaining health.

Our last contact was in May 2013 and Heather reported that she felt really good, as long as she continued to follow my health strategy. Her family also understood the link between certain foods and Heather's symptoms and they were quick to offer her a 'proper' meal, one which included different vegetable options when it was needed. She has had to make a concerted effort over a three-year period to be able to work and live without compromising one or the other. With both sound dietary advice and the results from the various non-invasive tests that we agreed upon to complete her holistic health investigation, Heather left my care with a greater understanding of how her personal health and medical history had contributed to her presenting symptoms back in 2010.

This newfound knowledge enabled her to see how powerful dietary choices can be in alleviating certain symptoms and how easy it is to incorporate this health strategy in her daily life. I encouraged Heather to choose foods that she could realistically include in her daily menu to make this health journey even easier to follow. Heather already enjoyed making meals and it was easy for her to continue investing time in the kitchen.

The ultimate test of any healthy eating strategy is to see if a patient can follow it long-term. Heather's response, after I contacted her in 2017 to ask for her permission to be included in this book, says it all:

"I had always eaten healthily and had a keen interest in preparing good quality food but I was surprised at how limited my diet had become, whilst I was struggling to work out which foods were upsetting me. I followed the diet religiously and soon realised that there was never a truer saying than 'You are what you eat!' If I stray from the diet at all, my friends and family know immediately and my weight reflects my food choices. I am convinced that I would have been worse by now if it wasn't for the excellent advice I had from Wilma and the balanced, varied diet that I now eat."

## Take-Home Message

➢ Fad diets *never* work, there is no quick fix.
➢ Learn to prepare, eat, and enjoy an array of vegetables.
➢ Vegetables contain essential nutrients.
➢ *All* the health agencies promote the inclusion of vegetables in the diet.
➢ If you are taking any form of medication, be aware of the side-effects.
➢ Feeling unusually tired? Ask your doctor for a blood test to assess your iron (ferritin) levels.
➢ Iron tablet not fixing your fatigue? Test your adrenal gland production of the stress hormone, cortisol.
➢ Forty years old, hormonal, with weight concerns? Ask your doctor for a complete
➢ thyroid blood test.

## Meal Ideas to Increase Vegetable Intake

### Breakfast
Egg omelette with chopped red pepper, fresh tomatoes, and courgette. Add cress when served.

### Lunch
Vegetable soup containing carrots, butternut, celery, sweetcorn, and chickpeas.

### Dinner
125 g grilled trout with sweet potato, kale, and asparagus.

**Condiments**

Add a tablespoon of good quality olive oil to raw and cooked vegetables. Other options can include flaxseed, walnut, avocado, and hempseed oils.

Refer to chapter 9 for a complete food list.

# Prepare Your Plate for Optimum Gut Health

## Jenni's Story

Jenni, a 26-year-old single lady, sought my help with facial acne and persisting IBS symptoms that started whilst she was taking her last round of prescribed acne medication.

*****

Jenni talks loud and fast, clearly very keen to tell her story and move towards a possible solution. She is the poster girl for rural England with her flowing blond hair, silken skin, light blue eyes, and her role at the British Association for Shooting and Conservation (BASC). Her fair classic English complexion is marred by visible acne on her delicate skin and it has been an uphill struggle since the age of 12, even before she reached puberty. As is the case with many female acne sufferers the medical recommendation was to introduce the oral contraceptive pill to address suspected hormonal imbalances. At the time of seeking my help, Jenni had been following this advice for 12 years and had also twice been prescribed an extensive treatment of Accutane (isotretinoin), containing a form of vitamin A to address skin conditions like *acne vulgaris*. She confesses that one of her greatest desires is to overcome this awful skin condition. To no longer have people stare at her face when she enters a room.

Her last treatment for this aesthetically distressing condition started a mere five years ago and only one year prior to that, Jenni began to notice that her gut was misbehaving with symptoms such as excess wind and diarrhoea, a classic tale of IBS. Jenni reveals that she always makes sure that she has a packet of antidiarrheal medication in her bag given that she often has an overwhelming urge to empty her bowels. She continues to explain that she would love to be able to go about her day-to-day activities without the constant worry of where the nearest toilet is because when her bowels start rumbling, there is no time to waste. Do you find yourself always asking where the nearest toilet is or only going to public places where you know that the amenities are plentiful? Being caught unawares is one of *the* most embarrassing experiences and many people would rather stay at home than risk this outcome.

When we investigated what Jenni was regularly eating we saw that she would often have a bowl of cereal, even for lunch and dinner. Jenni confesses to being a very poor cook and given that she lives alone it is not surprising that quick and easy options would be her preferred choices. Her diet was overwhelmingly concentrated on carbohydrates from cereal grains and consequently lacking in good quality protein and indispensable vegetables.

As you can see, her plate composition was far from ideal.

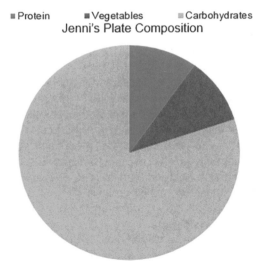

The ideal plate composition, in contrast, should consist of ½ **V**egetables, ¼ **P**rotein, and ¼ **C**arbohydrates.

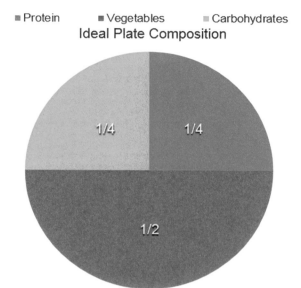

Protein ■ Vegetables ■ Carbohydrates

**Ideal Plate Composition**

1/4    1/4

1/2

Jenni was not following a fad diet because she wanted to lose weight, she was inadvertently following an exclusion diet, purely because it was convenient. And given that both the traditional food pyramid and the NHS Eatwell Guide encourage people to base the bulk of their diets around cereal grains and potatoes, Jenni did not see her meal choices as being contrary to the official health guidelines.

## The Role of Carbohydrates

Let us spend some time looking at the reasons why a carbohydrate-rich diet is not conducive to positive long-term health outcomes. Carbohydrates form a very important part of our meals because they are the main source of energy in most diets. In Asian cultures rice features predominantly, in Ireland potatoes reign supreme, in Italy pasta is the obvious option, and in most of the world, bread is the starch of choice. Jenni, like other perhaps single, busy people, and students on a tight budget, preferred breakfast cereal as her main carbohydrate to give her a quick and instant energy boost and to make light work of preparing meals.

To fully understand the body's energy needs let us also explore the journey from carbohydrate-rich foods to the end product of usable energy. Once eaten, carbohydrates are converted to glucose, or often referred to as sugar, through a series of intricate biological steps. The journey to a usable energy molecule, ATP (Adenosine TriPhosphate), does not end there and with the help of certain vitamins and enzymes, and a complex process involving multiple intermediate steps, we eventually end up with what biologists call the 'energy currency of life'. When we look at human biology we know we are exploring a very complex system.

Glucose is an indeed an easily available source of energy and is the body's preferred fuel source. When we do not consume adequate amounts of carbohydrates, our organs, especially the brain, start to suffer. The brain, arguably the hardest working organ in the human body, is like a newly hatched chick which demands constant feeding. That is why skipping meals often make people feel a little light-headed or dizzy. It is also one of the reasons why people who follow the Atkins, low carbohydrate, or the palaeolithic diet may feel unwell and lacking in energy at times.

When you look at images of the traditional food pyramid and the NHS Eatwell Plate you can see that the carbohydrate options include a variety of cereals, bread, pasta, rice, and potatoes. The concern with these visual images is that the focus is overwhelmingly in favour of breakfast cereals, bread, and wheat grain, so whilst it supports Jenni's choices, it clearly does not represent the optimal choices. If it did, Jenni should already be in peak physical condition. In most of our diets, the accompaniments of these options are either milk, butter or dairy-free spreads, and a tomato-based pasta sauce. A breakfast of cereal and milk, or buttered toast, is highly unlikely to make you reach for a vegetable or even a fruit. Lunchtime offerings of a sandwich are more likely to contain a slice of cold meat, cheese, or hummus rather than a variety of fresh salad ingredients. You might even be one of those people who would open up a sandwich and throw away the slice of tomato that might have been added. For most people, the much-anticipated pasta dish at dinner is served with either a cream sauce, something like a Carbonara, or tomato sauce, basil, and grated parmesan cheese or suitable vegan alternative. Adding up the numbers, this type of daily diet supplies a considerable amount of energy allowing the body to be ready for a good amount of physical exercise, especially for someone who is an athlete or who engages in high-intensity work activities. Even though Jenni works outdoors her energy demands cannot be deemed as higher than average.

## Are Food Sensitivities Just Another Fad?

The health concern for Jenni in terms of her plate composition, which by far favoured cereal grains, was linked with her presenting IBS symptoms. From a dietary point of view, enjoying wheat grains and popular breakfast cereals in abundance can be problematic because both wheat and corn form part of a select few foods that can negatively affect digestive function in many people. Other common problem foods include bovine (cow) dairy, soya, eggs, and some varieties of nuts and seeds. Jenni included two of those common problem foods at most meals, wheat and dairy (breakfast cereal and milk). So, in essence, her select food choices were contributing to her IBS symptoms, which is contrary to her belief that she had already been avoiding the suspected problem foods. We know that the gold standard test for food sensitivities is an elimination (oligoantigenic) diet and that process can be laborious and can extend over weeks or even months before results are collected. Patients run the risk of avoiding many essential food options because, after much trial and error, they are left with a meagre handful of options. Jenni insisted that we explore a more direct route and uncover exactly which foods were problematic via a blood test.

There are many tests on the market that claim to identify food intolerances, such as the very popular Vega test, hair analysis, and applied kinesiology. Like fad diets, these methods of testing are questionable, the evidence of efficacy is lacking, and even though it may be possible that a positive result can be indicative of a problematic food you should investigate further. Avoiding multiple foods and even food groups based on this type of result, for prolonged periods of time, can have significant negative consequences.

Results from food intolerance testing often indicate that you are eating a particular food or even multiple foods over and over again without much variation. The key to interpreting results is to see how it relates to your food choices. Address the findings by introducing a greater variety of foods and nutrient-dense alternatives, rather than summarily starting to avoid foods. For example, if you, like Jenni, eat a wheat-based cereal complemented with cow's milk every day, your best option is to introduce different cereal varieties such as oats, rice, and corn. Combine it with different milk alternatives and rotate your diet so that you can then give your body the chance to be optimally nurtured by a greater variety of options if you find you simply cannot abandon this traditional, no fuss, instant breakfast. The other alternative is to change your view on traditional breakfast to be more in line with the rest of the world, that is, those cultures that do not differentiate between breakfast, lunch, and dinner, food is food and is enjoyed regardless of the time of day. Breakfast in Costa Rica includes black beans and rice, which is complemented with avocado, fried ripe plantain and an assortment of cold meats. The Egyptians traditionally favour cooked fava beans with olive oil, lemon juice and garlic. In the Philippines, choices can include roasted suckling pig with fried rice. Perhaps a good start to a cold autumn morning would be a lentil and vegetable soup. For those individuals who do physically demanding work, a hearty beef soup with added vegetables could keep those mid-morning hunger pangs at bay. To optimise your health, it is worth venturing beyond your perception of what is 'normal'. Explore outside of your comfort zone and discover nutrient-dense breakfast options which help you maximise your health outcome. Often we are stuck in a certain eating rut, not because we dislike other options, but merely because this is the way we were raised and nobody ever suggested any alternatives. Jenni considered this advice and started enjoying savoury dishes and salads for breakfast with incredible results.

# The Facts Around Irritable Bowel Syndrome (IBS)

Given that Jenni's major symptoms were gut related, it is time to look at why IBS is receiving so much attention in the media. IBS has become a hot topic for conversation amongst healthcare professionals and unlike inflammatory bowel disease (IBD) this is not a disease, but rather termed a condition. This means that many patients are being told that they should just get on with their lives. The difficulties with IBS treatment start with the absence of a diagnostic tool and are exacerbated by a lack of specific medical protocols needed to successfully address the presenting symptoms, which in themselves can differ substantially between patients. Compare this to having a headache, where simply taking a headache tablet is all that is needed to fix the problem, for most people, most of the time. The medication on offer to treat IBS at best works for some people, only some of the time. When it comes to IBS, many patients have revealed that at the end of a long and tiresome road, after consulting with different physicians, having tried all the prescriptive digestive aids, they were referred to a behavioural therapist because the consensus is, 'it is *all* in your head'.

Patients experience different symptoms and given that there is not one standard diagnostic test, be it a blood test or an X-ray, and even a standardised protocol (a pill or a syrup) in place, trying to make sense of your IBS symptoms can be a minefield. If you look at the official criteria for IBS diagnosis you can be forgiven for ending up more confused at the end of your investigation.

**Table 2**. Rome IV criteria for diagnosing IBS

Patients who have had recurrent abdominal pain at least 1 day a week in the last 3 months associated with two or more of the following:

1. Related to defecation,
2. Associated with a change in frequency of stool,
3. Associated with a change in form (consistency) of stool.

IBS is one of the top 10 reasons why people seek primary care help and when that fails patients turn to alternative therapies. To date, few effective therapies have been identified despite the countless websites and blogs professing to hold the magic bullet, the unique product, *the* miracle cure. The situation has reached a stage where IBS is considered the most common functional digestive disorder affecting 10–20% of the adult population in several Western countries. Could there possibly be a link here with IBS and the standard Western diet or indeed the Western lifestyle? Despite these rising statistics, it is believed that a staggering 75% of patients suffering from IBS symptoms in the USA remain undiagnosed. If you have been suffering from IBS type symptoms you too have probably asked your doctor for help, finally gotten a referral to a gastroenterologist, had an endoscopy or colonoscopy and eventually, turned to the internet to get some form of relief. You might even have spent a small fortune on alternative therapies and still be baffled by your persisting gut irritation, which despite an initial brief period of relief, is back and continues to ruin your day.

What has been established without any doubt is that food choices are directly linked to gut function. Other possible factors include over the counter and prescription medication, lifestyle factors, and unwanted parasites or bacteria in the gut. Jenni's diet is clearly a major component and because she has never travelled to exotic locations or had food poisoning, suspecting a parasite or bacteria would seem inappropriate. To assume anything when dealing with a person whose gut is misbehaving without proper reason may prevent you from uncovering the root cause.

Jenni completed a comprehensive stool analysis and the results showed that she was one of the many people with unwanted parasites in her gut. Needless to say, Jenni was horrified to learn that there were parasites living in her gut, sharing her food, and ultimately making her unwell. Almost all my patients who have some skin affliction, be it eczema, psoriasis, rashes, or in Jenni's case, acne, have some kind of gut dysbiosis.

That means that there is something living in their gastrointestinal tract that should not be present, such as an abnormal amount of yeast, parasites, or bacteria. If you experience any skin problems, make sure that you get tested otherwise you will be spending years chasing the next wonder skin cream, embarking on yet another course of antibiotics, all yielding disappointing short-term results.

## Parasites and Bad Bacteria in the Modern Era

You might be wondering why some people have parasites or bacteria in their digestive tract and others do not. The bowel houses trillions of microorganisms which form two sides, one is present to protect your gut environment and the other could potentially cause you harm. Trillions of microorganisms, both good and bad, battle for the same space in which to grow. Like an old-fashioned pendulum scale, balance is reached when both sides carry equal amounts of weight. If one side increases, then the other side diminishes in numbers.

For optimal health, our goal is to maintain balance in the gut but this is challenged by a myriad of factors, such as:

- type of birth (naturally delivered babies have higher beneficial bacteria numbers compared to babies delivered via caesarean section),
- infant feeding practices (breast milk promote the growth of beneficial bacteria whereas infant formula still falls short of the gold standard, mother's milk),
- disease (coeliac or asthma),
- trauma,
- stress (including regular intense physical exercise),
- environment (toxic chemicals such as smoking or working with pesticides),
- antibiotic use,
- food choices (low plant fibre intake).

Pathogens and bad bacteria thrive in an environment rich in dietary starch, whereas beneficial bacteria do not. Beneficial flora prefers a different environment, supported by the intake of fibre in the form of vegetables and fruit. Recent focus on the human gut microbiome shows that not only is it imperative for good gut health to include fibre, what is crucial is the variety of vegetables and fruit consumed. The more different types of produce that you choose on a regular basis, the more likely you are to cultivate a rich diversity of bacteria, which is being shown to optimise health. So food choices play a big part in gut behaviour.

## What Happened to Jenni?

Jenni's food choices remain our main concern because her diet is severely lacking in essential nutrients, which she can get from vegetables and good protein sources. Her first challenge is to take a list of nutrient-dense food options with her when buying groceries. This enables her to choose specific options and steer clear of the breakfast cereals, which can take up a whole aisle in most supermarkets. If you head out to buy groceries without a definitive list, you run the risk of ambling and have those nutrient void temptations catch your eye and end up in the basket at the expense of choosing nutrient-dense food. Similarly, if you ever shop on an empty stomach, close to a mealtime, you might be more tempted to satisfy your cravings rather than focus on optimal meal ingredients. For Jenni, her need to buy only a select few carbohydrates driven by convenience and bad habits changes to nutrient-dense carbohydrate options because those are now on her shopping list. Jenni also does not need to buy copious amounts of these newly discovered nutrient-dense carbohydrates because she understands that her energy needs are not higher than average.

**Table 3**. Nutrient-dense carbohydrate choices
Amaranth
Barley
Buckwheat
Millet
Oats
Polenta (Ground maize)
Potato
Quinoa
Rice (Basmati, Black, Brown, Wild)
Sorghum

Jenni might never become an accomplished chef but she is encouraged to become more comfortable in the kitchen. The more time you invest in preparing nutritious foods, the more time you can spend enjoying life rather than worrying about where the nearest toilet is.

Three months after Jenni's health journey began she reported that her IBS had noticeably improved and as an added bonus had noticed that her cellulite had vanished as well. Jenni was set on optimising her health and became quite creative with her meals by avoiding the identified food culprits and incorporating nutrient-dense alternatives. I daresay she probably inspired a few of her circle of friends in the process when invited to summer barbecues and get-togethers. Her skin also responded positively to the dietary changes even though it took longer to completely heal than her IBS. Seven years later, after walking down the aisle, the picture of a radiant bride, she happily reports:

"Wilma was fantastic, not only was she a brilliant listener, she really took into account all the factors affecting me – my diet, my hectic work and social life – and she really helped me to rethink my attitude towards food and lifestyle. Not only can I eat all the foods now I once had to avoid, I am much better at managing my diet, taking everything in moderation, thinking about what my body needs, not necessarily what I fancy. My skin improved and my IBS is all but forgotten. Sometimes, we are our own worst enemy and Wilma helped me to see that just by changing a few things and considering what you eat, you can live a normal, healthy lifestyle and enjoy all that it brings."

## Take-Home Message

➢ Refined breakfast cereals, pastries, bread, crisps and biscuits will *never* be part of a nutritious diet.

➢ Carbohydrates or starches should not make up the bulk of your diet.

➢ If you have any skin condition, be it psoriasis, acne, eczema, or rosacea, investigate your gut health.

➢ If you have any signs of IBS, test your gut environment to rule out the presence of pathogens.

➢ Test your gut to assess your level and diversity of good gut bacteria if any of the following apply to you:

Born via caesarean section,
Not breastfed or were but not for very long,
Have any stress in your life,
Were ever prescribed antibiotic treatment,
Have had food poisoning or traveller's diarrhoea,
Exercise regularly with great intensity.

➢ If you suspect that you are sensitive to some foods either opt for an elimination (oligoantigenic) diet or choose a blood test to identify the offending foods.

## Meal Ideas for Optimum Gut Health

**Breakfast**
Porridge oats (made with water only) with 2 tablespoons of pumpkin seeds, sunflower seeds or ground flax seeds

**Lunch**
Humus/chicken/smoked salmon sandwich on rye or gluten-free bread with lettuce, tomato, carrot, cucumber, bell pepper

**Dinner**
1 baked potato / sweet potato with 125 g tinned/fresh tuna
Mixed green salad dressed with 1 tablespoon extra-virgin cold pressed oil

**Condiments**
Add a tablespoon of good quality olive oil to raw and cooked vegetables. Other options can include flaxseed, walnut, avocado, and hempseed oils.

Refer to chapter 9 for a complete food list.

# Prepare Your Plate to Address Bowel Disease

## Lawrence's Story

On Saturday the 7 August 2010, I met Lawrence, a single 20-year-old, and his mother, who made the appointment for her son. Lawrence had been diagnosed with Crohn's disease, an incurable inflammatory bowel disease (IBD). Both he and his mother were very concerned about his recent dramatic weight loss.

*****

Few people realise how big the buildings along Harley Street are and how many consulting rooms are hidden from street view. My office is a fair walk from the front door – situated at the back of the building, quiet and discreet – and is, therefore, the perfect spot for engaging in sensitive discussions about a person's personal health, and often their life stories. When I meet Lawrence at the entrance to the building, I am taken aback by how emaciated he looks. He has piercing blue eyes, a hint of stubble, and short, shaven, jet-black hair. He and his mother both look tense. As he enters, I notice how slowly and arduously Lawrence moves. I wonder how he will manage the stairs and a long walk to my consulting room. As a mother, I have a strong desire to lend him a helping hand, and for a brief moment, I compare his gait with that of a person decades his senior.

Lawrence suffers from Crohn's disease, an inflammatory bowel disease (IBD) for which there is no cure; the inevitable outcome, for 100% of patients, is surgery. He has an excellent patient-physician relationship with his consultant gastroenterologist. He is also under the care of a registered dietician, who is in charge of his nutritional needs. This dietician's recommendations focused on helping Lawrence put on weight, at all cost, and included a liquid meal-replacement post-diagnosis, followed by the Lofflex diet (Low Fat Fibre Limitation Exclusion Diet). Despite being under the finest medical care, Lawrence continued to react badly to certain foods; because his weight was plummeting at an alarming rate, he sought additional nutritional help. At this point Lawrence, who stands 185 cm (6 foot 1 inches) tall, weighs a meagre 55 kg (8 stone 9 pounds), giving him a BMI of only 16. An optimal diet is desperately needed to ensure that Lawrence's future will have a positive health outcome. Unfortunately, the recommended meal-replacement option, Ensure®, (which was chosen to help Lawrence gain weight) is not having the desired effect, but making his symptoms worse.

Let us have a look at Lawrence's plate composition at the time when he came to the clinic.

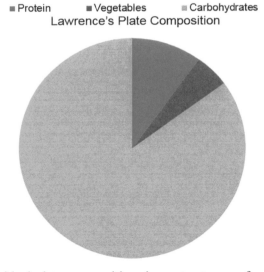

The ideal plate composition, in contrast, even for a person diagnosed with IBD should consist of ½ **Vegetables**, ¼ **Protein**, and ¼ **Carbohydrates**.

## Ideal Plate Composition

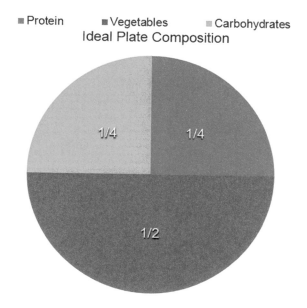

Lawrence is not adventurous with his diet. Until now, he has been heavily reliant on refined carbohydrates and sugar. This is not uncommon for someone living the student life; oddly enough, it is perfectly in line with the traditional recommendations for weight increase. Patients who are severely underweight are encouraged to eat as many carbohydrates (in the form of bread, pastries, pasta, biscuits, and sweets) as possible to help put on weight. Like the fad diets which ultimately focus only on weight loss, this eating strategy only focuses on weight increase. The long-term nutritional status or health outcome is ignored because weight, yet again, is the only focus. Of course, being underweight is a health concern; however, if we lose sight of optimum nutritional status, then we are ignoring a crucial part of health therapy.

## What Is Crohn's Disease?

Unlike IBS (which many people suffer from), an IBD like Crohn's disease can lead to death, making it a very serious disease indeed. It is no wonder that Lawrence's mother was so concerned for her son's long-term health: he had not even celebrated his 21$^{st}$ birthday yet. Can you imagine the impact that such a diagnosis, especially at this young age, can have on your overall outlook on life? Lawrence had not yet completed his undergraduate university education; it now looked as if living away from home in university accommodation might no longer possible. A bitter pill for any young, motivated person to swallow.

Let us explore what Crohn's disease is and how it can affect nutrient uptake from food. Crohn's disease is a debilitating inflammatory bowel disease mainly affecting the latter or end part of the small intestine and the entire large bowel (colon). Interestingly enough, we still have no idea why some people are affected, even though there is a noticeable increase in the number of people affected. Some medics hypothesise that changes in beneficial gut bacteria, early exposure to antibiotic medication, a typical high-fat, sugar-rich, North American diet, and low levels of vitamin D may be triggers. Cases of a sort previously unheard of, involving children as young as 5, have been reported; there appears to be a significant increase in paediatric IBD, particularly in Canada, which has the highest rates.

The areas in the bowel that are affected by IBD are the very parts where nutrients are extracted from the food we eat. The process whereby food is converted into absorbable nutrients occurs exclusively in the bowel. There, carbohydrate-rich foods are broken down into glucose molecules, essential for energy production. Protein molecules are extracted and released to build muscle and aid growth and repair. A host of vitamins and minerals are collected to help your body function optimally. Clearly, when the bowel becomes inflamed, a whole array of biological functions is negatively affected.

Even though the first mention in the scientific literature of Crohn's disease dates back to 1903, treatment is still largely focused around medication to minimise inflammation, and surgery, where parts of the bowel are removed. In terms of lifestyle factors, stress and smoking both play a major role. If you are currently smoking, lead a stressful life, and experience severe gut symptoms, please ask your doctor to investigate further. With all diseases, the sooner you start treatment the better the outcome.

Fortunately, Lawrence does not smoke, unlike so many of his peers. We are all familiar with tales of university students drinking cheap alcohol, eating budget food, and recovering from late nights by sleeping until midday, once they are away from the prying eyes and judgmental opinions of their parents and guardians. To ensure that Lawrence could continue to live away from mom's help in the kitchen, we first needed to identify exactly which foods were exacerbating his symptoms, namely, diarrhoea, stomach cramps, eczema, and lack of energy. Whilst the best method to identify food sensitivities will always be the gold standard elimination (oligoantigenic) diet, sometimes it is very helpful to opt for a quicker route by completing a blood test. This was the most obvious choice for Lawrence; his weight loss was so severe that time was of the essence. Lawrence's long list of positively tested food culprits was not surprising, because certain food groups have already been identified as problematic for Crohn's disease sufferers.

**Table 4.** Common problematic food for Crohn's disease patients

Corn(maize)
Dairy
Legumes
Nuts and seeds
Wheat
Raw fruit and vegetables

*This list of foods may not apply to all Crohn's disease patients. Individual assessment is, therefore, necessary.*
However, we also identified a couple of unsuspected foods and immediately discussed how best he might maintain an optimal diet without including the culprits. In order to help Lawrence to understand the importance of adopting a more positive relationship with food, it was important to emphasise both the positive and negative aspects, which he alone would experience. Those around him did not have Crohn's disease; however, despite his anger at being different, he remained the master of his destiny. His mother is very supportive, so

financial concerns around food purchases were not an issue; this meant that Lawrence could avoid the nutrient-void budget choices, and invest in better quality food instead.

When someone is as severely underweight as Lawrence, my health strategy is to include foods such as oily fish to support healthy weight gain. The additional benefit of adding salmon, trout, tuna, mackerel, halibut, and sardines to the diet is that each is an excellent source of protein. Lawrence's diet was very limited on the protein front, which is an essential macronutrient for growth and repair and helps to build strong, healthy muscle as well.

## The Issue with Meal-Replacement Products

So, what is nutritionally wrong with the Ensure® meal-replacement products, commonly used in hospitals, and given to Lawrence to support weight gain? The short answer is just to list the first few ingredients: corn syrup, corn maltodextrin, sugar, and corn oil. Remember that a diet rich in sugar does not help the growth of healthy gut bacteria; conversely, it provides the perfect environment for bad bacteria. Secondly, the carbohydrate content is significantly high, ranging from 34 g to 44 g of which the sugar composition ranges from 13 g to 20 g.

Then there is the fact that the meal-replacement products contain milk and soy ingredients, all hyper allergenic components; this results in a product that is extremely ill-suited to a patient who has just been diagnosed with Crohn's disease. Finally, when we look at the nutritional composition we see that the protein content is low (between 9 g and 20 g per serving, depending on the chosen product).

The oily fish that I recommended for Lawrence contain protein ranging from 19 g–25 g (per 100 g serving). They are also rich in healthy, unsaturated fats, which play an essential role in reducing inflammation. IBD is an *inflammatory* disease of the gastrointestinal tract, so choosing food with anti-inflammatory properties is vital for addressing inflammation in the gut, the epicentre of digestion. Unlike the carbohydrate-rich meal replacements, not one of the oily fish options contains any carbohydrates. In essence, these delicious real food options are crammed with healthy protein and essential fats, an optimal combination when supporting healthy weight gain and addressing inflammation.

It could be pointed out that this range of meal-replacement products contain 26 vitamins and minerals, and is low in fibre, in keeping with what the Lofflex diet aims to achieve. Furthermore, it might be said, fibre, especially from grains and legumes, can be an irritant in the gastrointestinal tract of an IBD patient, which can exacerbate presenting symptoms. However, emerging research clearly states that this approach is archaic and detrimental to the patient, given that the risk of colon cancer is significantly increased when diets are short of vegetable fibre.

Sugar is a major irritant in the gut. My advice to all IBD patients is to completely avoid all junk food, biscuits, sweets, and other confectionery (options traditionally recommended to underweight patients to aid quick weight increase). This is also the reason why I am completely against every one of the meal-replacement products which have sugar (and variations thereof) as the first three listed ingredients. IBD patients can obtain optimum nutrition from real food, just like people who are not affected by this inflammatory disease. The better alternative to sugar-laden meal replacements would be to enjoy liquidised, nutrient-dense soups, especially when a patient has difficulty chewing or experiences reduced appetite. When endeavouring to minimise inflammation in the gut of an IBD patient, one must be very vigilant and informative when recommending what the patient should choose to dine on. Someone like Lawrence, who has just been diagnosed with a life-long disease, is in a very vulnerable physical and emotional state and deserves sound nutritional advice in line with positive health outcomes. This advice cannot be merely a plan to put on the pounds in the shortest time possible.

## Facing and Overcoming Dietary Challenges

Lawrence is a very motivated young man. He took on board the simple health strategies that I proposed without any (overt) resistance. Because we had a tested list of food culprits and not one vegetable was included on it, we proceeded to add safe, palatable, cooked, vegetable options. There is no sound argument for ignoring the many health benefits of a diet rich in plant fibre, the kind of fibre gained from vegetables.

These dietary changes were easy to incorporate in Lawrence's daily routine. He soon realised that he could prepare nutritious meals, even without his mother's input! In fact, on the second visit, his mother told me that the whole family was eating healthier thanks to my advice. To have familial support when you embark on a diet that is significantly different from your previous regimen is invaluable, because you do not feel left out, and your dining companions reap similar benefits as well. A mere two weeks after the first consultation Lawrence reported that his symptoms had already greatly improved with no more diarrhoea and only occasional abdominal pain. The blisters in his mouth felt much better which meant he could enjoy food more. When your mouth is sensitive, it restricts the types of food that you can enjoy without experiencing pain. Lawrence's (very concerned) mother was so angry at the treatment that her son had received prior to seeing me that she had written a strongly worded letter, airing her concerns and displeasure, addressed to the parties in question.

My health strategy was so easy to incorporate that Lawrence returned to university in the summer of that year, and fended for himself in the kitchen, very successfully indeed. The road back was not easy, and I had to point out that he had made such great improvements in such a short space of time that every step from now on would help him cement his long-term health. It is one thing to hear these words from your mother, and quite another coming from your nutrition consultant. The realisation that he cannot join his peers in any pub or restaurant without risk was a hard one to accept, but by April 2011 his inflammation markers (tested by his consultant gastroenterologist) were almost back to normal. This reinforced the fact that his hard work and sacrifices were paying dividends. In his own words:

"I can't believe how something as simple as altering my diet has ultimately changed my life! When I first met you I genuinely felt my Crohn's Disease was getting so bad I'd need to be admitted into a hospital, and yet 6 months on from taking your dietary advice I'm healthier and more symptom-free than I've ever been! I've learnt that you can indeed be healthy and live a normal life despite living with an illness, and for that, I am truly grateful!

## The Effects of Stress for a Crohn's Patient

Life throws many challenges our way and sometimes they turn out to be very stressful. For someone like Lawrence, who already suffered from unsettling bowel behaviour, stress can have a very noticeable effect. His upcoming university exams resulted in minor flare-ups and elicited some serious self-doubt. The nature of any IBD is that you cannot predict the outcome and a patient can live in constant fear of relapse, which can mean hospitalisation and probably surgical intervention. It has been said that patients who live with chronic illnesses experience a 'loss of self', which makes the ultimate goal of any IBD patient to achieve a 'new normal'. For many sufferers, it can mean that you become the disease or condition; because those around you cannot truly understand the true nature of this illness, it can mean social seclusion and isolation (least of all because you are constantly aware of where the toilet facilities are, just in case). There is no cure for inflammatory bowel disease and that is the hardest part for any sufferer to make peace with. They must resign to a life ruled by long-term medication and the constant worry that surgery is the rule rather than the exception.

## The Challenges of Gaining Weight

Given that the gut environment is almost constantly inflamed, it is difficult for IBD patients to absorb nutrients from their diet and, as a result, weight gain can be a lifelong struggle. A Crohn's patient already has a negative relationship with food due to the many exclusions necessary to reduce inflammation in the gut. If you constantly worry that your food may make you lose control of your bowels, you become considerably vigilant about what you actually put in your mouth. Where another person may just increase food intake to boost weight, a Crohn's patient cannot adopt the same approach, and Lawrence remained unhappy about his inability to bulk up. Another symptom of IBD is fatigue, so you have to be sensible in what activities you are willing to invest energy in. By being unable to absorb nutrients from your diet you also limit the amount of energy the body can produce. Add to that the multitude of problematic food options, and you can see how much of life this disease can interfere with. The type of exercise a patient embarks on can play a big part in both conserving energy and helping to build muscle. For Lawrence, some exercise options were not ideal and I encouraged him to speak to a qualified trainer to help him devise a suitable weight training programme. Weight training or lifting focuses on specific muscle activity and the slow repeatable exercises involved conserve important energy stores unlike running or cross training which can make you feel drained quite quickly.

## What Happened to Lawrence?

By the end of 2012, Lawrence was completely medication- and eczema-free. He was in a very good place in terms of health. Not only did he complete his undergraduate degree, he later successfully gained his master's degree. My simple health strategy was realistic enough even for an unadventurous Crohn's patient to incorporate and to see the benefits. Lawrence furthermore maintained this sensible dietary plan long-term; he is no longer the same person as the one shuffling along the long corridor back in 2010.

As with all IBD patients, Lawrence did eventually have surgery in October 2015 where a staggering 40 cm of his bowel was removed. Despite this unfortunate development, Lawrence successfully published a research article in 2016 which investigated the experience of living with IBD. In the article, he highlighted the challenges faced by sufferers of this incurable disease. For many IBD patients, a diagnosis can result in taking on fewer work commitments, but Lawrence decided that he was going to embark on a long road of academic studies. He gained a PhD in 2017 and sent me this update:

"Health-wise, I actually ended up needing surgery in October 2015. I was doing pretty well on diet alone for a fair few years after seeing you but I think just wear and tear over time had taken its toll and they had to remove a section of bowel that was too damaged and narrow. Very rough couple of weeks in the hospital and quite a battle to recover afterwards but things are definitely better now."

## Take-Home Message

➢ Stop smoking.
➢ If you have been diagnosed with an incurable disease, accept and respect your diagnosis.
➢ Long-term medication is designed to ameliorate symptoms. Diet is a very powerful ally.
➢ Learn to prepare, eat, and enjoy nutritious food.
➢ Food sensitivity exploration is only viable via either elimination (oligoantigenic) diet or blood test.
➢ Meal-replacement formulas are not superior to nature's own, real food in the long-term.
➢ Breastfeeding infants for at least six months offer excellent long-term gut protective properties.
➢ For Crohn's disease be cautious with the following foods:
wheat,
corn,
dairy,
legumes,
nuts and seeds,
raw vegetables and fruit.

## Meal Ideas for Crohn's Patients

### Breakfast
Quinoa or millet flakes with coconut milk and some finely ground pumpkin seeds

### Lunch
Turkey or chicken salad (fennel and avocado) with a few new potatoes

### Dinner
Finely cut stir-fried vegetables (chestnut mushrooms, carrots, Chinese leaf, asparagus) with 125g of grilled mackerel

### Condiments

Add a tablespoon of good quality olive oil to raw and cooked vegetables. Other options can include flaxseed, avocado, and hempseed oils.

Refer to chapter 9 for a complete food list.

# Prepare Your Plate for
# Hormonal Balance

## Cherisse's Story

On a beautiful summer's evening in July 2012, Cherisse sought my help in addressing her symptoms of Pre-Menstrual Syndrome (PMS) and to additionally support her energy levels which are constantly challenged by her hectic work life.

*****

When I open the heavy wooden door to welcome Cherisse I could be forgiven for thinking that she is a heptathlete. Her flawless skin accentuates her perfectly sculpted physique, and her exuberant personality paves the way for a most enjoyable encounter. It turns out Cherisse is an athlete but not the way I imagined, she is an internationally acclaimed drummer, a professional musician. So what brings this healthy looking woman to my clinic? It turns out that being female has an obvious downside when you have a physically demanding job. PMS, which makes an unwelcome appearance every month with some regularity for most women between the ages of 11 and 50, can noticeably interfere with a super demanding travel diary and energy demands.

## The History of Pre-Menstrual Syndrome (PMS)

Let us take a little look at the history of PMS as documented in the scientific literature. In 1931 Frank T. Robert, a gynaecologist at Mount Sinai Hospital in New York, published one of the first papers on the subject of Pre-Menstrual

Tension, also termed Pre-Menstrual Syndrome. His treatment strategy included dehydration therapy (using diuretics such as coffee, tea, and calcium) and in extreme cases, surgical removal of the ovaries. Cherisse and I would not consider any one of these drastic measures, not least of all because she is so young. Some reports say that as many as 95% of women of childbearing age suffer from PMS and Cherisse's symptoms of depression, mood swings, tearfulness, inability to make decisions, headaches, irritability, communication difficulties, spots, sensitive and thin skin, lack of perspective, bloating, and chocolate cravings were all in line with the common PMS symptom tick box list. Fortunately, only about 5–10% of women describe their PMS symptoms as debilitating and Cherisse was not one of them even though it could noticeably affect both her work and social life. Just because the medical community does not diagnose your hormonal imbalance as debilitating does not mean you will not at times feel like these regularly occurring symptoms are ruining your life, both in terms of productivity and enjoyment. When you are forced to take a few days off each month because you are in severe pain, desperately tired, or abnormally irrational, you can be forgiven for envying your male counterparts.

When we look at the causes of PMS, what does history tell us? The exact origin of PMS is still not well understood and historically it was seen as an imaginary disease. This meant that too many women suffered in silence. Clearly, until women were allowed to enter the workplace our male counterparts were a little oblivious of female hormonal issues and the patriarchal medical profession did not deem 'female hysterics' of great medical interest other than mental instability. We are uncovering many factors that exacerbate PMS of which smoking is a major consideration. Research done on the topic of PMS shows that the younger a woman is when she starts to smoke, the more severe the PMS symptoms will be. So, if you are smoking to reduce appetite or induce relaxation, now is the time to explore other avenues from which you can reap the benefits without putting your health at risk. Another important lifestyle factor is exercise, shown to diminish the severity of PMS. The added benefit of regular exercise, from yoga to marathon running, is weight maintenance, stress reduction, and the positive effects it exerts on mood, one of the primary complaints associated with PMS. As with many conditions, being overweight is associated with more severe symptoms and in extreme cases, a major risk factor for premature death. When you next assess your weight, be honest and if you are overweight make a concerted effort to lose the excess pounds. Do not choose one of those diets that promise instant results, instead opt for a strategy, like the plate composition, which focuses both on weight management and positive long-term health outcome.

## Physical Activity and Health

Cherisse, aged 25, is a mere 156 cm (5 foot 1 inch) tall and maintains a very healthy weight because she is incredibly active. Being overweight or indeed underweight can be a factor in hormonal health. Fortunately Cherisse is a non-smoker because smoking plays a significant role in exacerbating symptoms of PMS. With Cherisse there was something else at play and I recommended that we investigate her adrenal gland activity to see if there were any irregularities with regards to her stress hormone secretion. This is the first step in addressing hormonal inconsistencies because the stress hormone, cortisol, plays a significant part in disrupting female hormone secretion. Cherisse has an incredibly demanding physical job and it easy to see how this type of physiological stress can impact on PMS symptoms.

Diet plays an essential role in ameliorating PMS symptoms. For women of menstruating age who engage in physically demanding activities, such as competitive sport, or lead lives dictated by stressful events (motherhood, full-time employment, and caregiving, to name but a few) additional investigation and support is needed. Food choices will go a long way towards addressing PMS symptoms but sometimes that alone may not be sufficient to address the underlying issues.

Let us have a look at Cherisse's plate composition to see which food groups she was choosing.

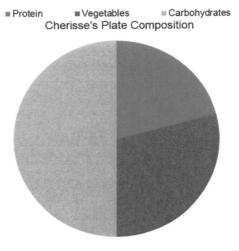

The ideal plate composition, in contrast, even for a person who is extremely active should consist of ½ **Vegetables**, ¼ **Protein**, and ¼ **Carbohydrates**.

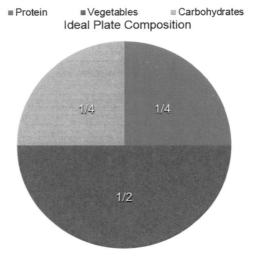

You might think that Cherisse's plate composition was perfectly in line with her demanding physical work. Surely, someone who is that active needs a considerable amount of carbohydrates in line with the traditional food pyramid and the NHS EatWell guide recommendations. That assumption is incorrect. When we look at stress and PMS related symptoms, excess carbohydrates or starchy food can make the symptoms worse. For these types of presenting symptoms, it is better to include half a plate of vegetables, which include starch options such as sweet potatoes and corn on the cob, instead of an abundance of refined carbohydrate-rich cereal grains. The reason for this is that vegetables are not only packed with essential vitamins and minerals, but they also include valuable fibre to promote regular bowel movements. Many breakfast cereals are indeed fortified with added vitamins and minerals but opting for wholesome vegetables should always be considered first given that these choices have formed part of the human diet a lot longer than boxed breakfast options.

## Female Hormones During the Reproductive Years

To fully understand what happens in a woman's body when she menstruates, let us look at how the different hormones interact. When we consider female hormonal imbalances we are mostly focused on two hormones, progesterone and oestrogen. Women do secrete testosterone, the hormone mostly associated with our male counterparts due to its role in lean muscle development and increased muscular strength. The same hormone that is believed to give female athletes a competitive edge over their rivals, but let us leave that Pandora's box unopened.

The most common findings in women with PMS is that the ratio between these two female hormones is overwhelmingly in favour of oestrogen (oestradiol to be specific). During the luteal or secretory phase, roughly in the middle of your monthly cycle, progesterone secretion should ideally be at its peak. At this point, oestrogen secretion should be low in comparison. Progesterone is the hormone that prepares the womb for pregnancy and prolonged high levels occur when an egg is successfully fertilised during ovulation. When the egg is not fertilised but released during the bleeding phase, both progesterone and oestrogen levels are at their lowest. The cycle is then repeated until a woman ceases to have regular menstrual bleeding at the time of menopause.

A woman of menstruating age, who suffers from PMS symptoms, conversely might produce significantly more oestrogen in comparison to progesterone during the luteal phase. This anomaly is what makes PMS symptoms more prominent.

**Table 5**. The different phases of the average menstrual cycle

| Phase | Average starting day (Assuming a 28-day cycle) | Average end day |
|---|---|---|
| Menstrual phase or bleeding phase. | 1 | 4 |
| Follicular phase (also known as the proliferative phase) where oestrogen levels are normally at its peak. | 5 | 13 |
| Ovulation (not strictly a phase, but an event dividing the phases). | 14 | 14 |
| Luteal phase (also known as the secretory phase) where progesterone is normally high to prepare for a possible pregnancy. | 15 | 26 |
| Ischemic phase (some sources group this with the secretory phase) where both oestrogen and progesterone are at their lowest. | 27 | 28 |

## What Are Some of the Obvious Signs and Symptoms Associated with PMS?

### Physical discomforts:
- Fluid retention
- Weight gain
- Sore or tender breasts
- Headaches
- Fatigue
- Nausea
- Insomnia or excessive sleep
- Abdominal cramps
- Muscle, joint, or back pain

**Negative effects:**

- Tension or anxiety
- Increased appetite or food cravings
- Irritability, even towards loved ones
- Depression or sadness not associated with grieving or loss
- Feelings of hopelessness
- Restlessness
- Tearfulness
- Anger
- Feeling overwhelmed

**Impaired cognitive function or performance:**

- Difficulty concentrating
- Distractibility
- Forgetfulness
- Confusion
- Mood swings
- Temper outbursts
- Accident prone
- Poor motor coordination
- Impulsiveness

The noticeable physical signs during the bleeding stage are heavy, clotty periods accompanied by abdominal pain, which may last longer than the average 3–5 days. Depression or low mood, associated with the menstrual cycle, is another clinical giveaway. Progesterone is considered the feel-good hormone and low levels may exacerbate symptoms of depressive mood. If you identify with any of these symptoms and feel that your PMS is ruining your enjoyment of life, have your hormone levels tested.

## Excess Oestrogen, Your Liver, and Detoxification

Hormone imbalances affect other organs, noticeably the biggest internal organ in the human body, the liver. An excess of oestrogen (associated with excess body weight and dietary choices) not only disrupt hormone stasis it can cause *cholestasis*, commonly known as 'sluggish liver'. The liver plays an important role in many metabolic processes particularly detoxification. The liver detoxification process is not just one reaction, it occurs in two phases. Phase I, orchestrated by cytochrome P450 enzymes, initiates the detoxification process by combining chemical breakdown reactions (oxidation, reduction, hydrolysis, hydration, and dehalogenation) and nutrients (vitamin B3, B6, B12, folic acid, to name a few) to expose toxins, make them water-soluble and therefore ready to be excreted via the urine. This phase is activated when internal toxins or environmental substances (xenobiotics such as pollutants, tobacco smoke, and medication) are detected. Oestrogen is viewed by the body as a potentially dangerous toxin, unlike progesterone, and also activates phase I detoxification. The higher your exposure to environmental toxins and the more excess oestrogen circulates in the bloodstream, the greater the burden on your liver. The circulating levels of oestrogen is an accumulation of that which you produce in your ovaries and exogenous sources (xenoestrogens). Pesticides, herbicides, hormones used for commercial livestock treatment, and the oral contraceptive pill all contribute to your xenoestrogen load. If you suffer from PMS, it seems prudent to minimise your exposure to xenoestrogens by limiting your intake of non-organic produce, meat, and dairy products and to discuss alternative methods of birth control with your gynaecologist.

Phase II, the conjugation pathway, proceeds when certain molecules (glucuronic acid, sulfate, glutathione, amino acids, acetic acid, and methyl groups) are added to the toxins broken down in phase I. Both these phases require adequate, specific nutrients gained from food (particularly plant fibre and protein), and energy to get the ball rolling, so to speak. If you are malnourished and suffer from fatigue, your detoxification abilities can be greatly impaired. Fasting or skipping meals is not an ideal way to detoxify. Note that excess oestrogen and stored toxins can result in many unexpected symptoms when you lose weight because they are released into the bloodstream and without successful elimination, your liver is burdened with this arduous task yet again.

A further complication occurs when phase I activity is higher than phase II. This imbalance can result in fat-soluble toxins building up in your body and being stored in the adipose (fat) tissue due to sub-optimal excretion. Imagine this imbalance like rush hour traffic where a bottle-neck situation arises leading to long tailbacks. For the kidneys to eliminate waste material, the toxins need to be water-soluble. Think of a drop of oil, it does not mix with water, it merely floats on top. If your kidneys are unable to excrete waste products, those toxins will remain in your body and bring forth a host of unexpected symptoms.

Patients on long-term medication are regularly screened for impaired liver function as prescription drugs put extra strain on the liver whose major function is to ensure that toxins are not reabsorbed. Similarly, women who binge drink are warned about the possible impact that alcohol can have on liver function and are encouraged to drink in moderation. When you are stressed and desperate to unwind at the end of a long working day you might automatically reach for a glass of wine when you get home. That glass of wine can have such a positive effect on a stressed woman's mood that one glass can potentially turn into two or more per night. The additional strain that alcohol and medication place on the liver can mean your sex hormones remain unbalanced, making PMS symptoms worse.

A little-known fact is that an impaired or challenged liver detoxification pathway can result in unwanted waste products lingering in the intestines, the site where nutrients from food are absorbed. The longer toxins remain in the body, the more likely they are at being absorbed. This is one of the reasons why healthcare professionals are so eager to address symptoms of constipation with patients at risk. People with irregular bowel movements, who can skip days or even weeks before emptying their bowels, are holding onto this unwanted waste, the perfect breeding ground for bad bacteria in the gut. When we refer to waste material, it is always better removed from the body than left in the gut because once excreted, it is no longer a potential health risk. The best antidote to sluggish bowel movements is plant fibre in the form of vegetables, legumes, and wholegrain cereals such as millet, quinoa, black, brown or wild rice, rye, and sorghum.

The added benefit of regular bowel movements is that you feel lighter and definitely less bloated, another common complaint.

## The Link Between Female Hormones and Stress

What may not be apparent is that anomalies associated with the stress hormone, cortisol, can directly affect the sex hormones and Cherisse agreed to have this area investigated via a salivary adrenal stress test. Simply put, when you are stressed or engaged in extreme physical activities, your female sex hormones (oestrogen and progesterone) may not be as well balanced compared to when you are calm, composed, and relaxed. Sub-optimal levels of cortisol disrupt oestrogen and progesterone secretion and it is best to investigate adrenal gland health before considering oestrogen or progesterone therapy. For many women, being stressed coincides with their cravings for empty calories in the form of highly processed or refined snack food such as crisps, biscuits, chocolate, energy drinks, alcohol, and coffee. The longer you are exposed to a continued level of physiological stress, the more likely your PMS symptoms are to become bothersome. Women who suffer from PMS may experience more intense symptoms in a work environment where stress is the order of the day. You might not be able to change your work environment or the other stresses in your life, but you can change your diet. Make sure that you have nutrient-dense meals within easy reach so that you can minimise these unwanted side-effects that are heightened by incorrect food choices. Being prepared also helps you veer away from temptation, a strong factor in an environment where edibles on offer are less than ideal and bountiful.

Cherisse finds herself in an environment where alcohol, junk food, coffee, and sugary snacks are omnipresent. When on tour, travelling by bus during the day and performing until late in the evening for weeks on end, the allure of a quick energy boost food or drink option is strong. Being at the mercy of someone else to provide food and drink means it can be difficult to avoid what is on offer. Similar to an office environment where the tradition is to bring a cake for everyone to enjoy on your birthday or indeed have a biscuit tin present all the time. Too many people have come to believe that a cup of tea (or coffee) and a biscuit is one item. A break is an excellent way to move away from your desk and for most people that quick sugar rush, in the form of sweetened tea, cake and biscuits, is what helps them through their working day. For someone who may be more inclined to pile on the pounds, this comfort break habit can have a very negative impact on their weight. Emerging research is casting doubt on the idea that some people can be fat and yet remain fit. It seems that excess weight is a major long-term health concern regardless of a person's current state of health. Minimising the temptation to indulge in empty calories (non-essential edibles), is the obvious choice whether you suffer from PMS or not.

For Cherisse, we want to make sure that any excess oestrogen is excreted (via the urine and faeces) so that she can maintain a healthy hormonal balance to minimise her symptoms of PMS. Choosing unrefined food options rich in plant fibre, inclusive of high protein, void of empty calories, that conform to the ideal plate composition, was the only logical solution.

## What Happened to Cherisse?

Cherisse has a unique lifestyle. Given that she is travelling so much for months on end, it is unrealistic to expect her to always be near a well-equipped kitchen or even the most basic of cooking facilities. Any recommendations need to take these factors into account so that the health strategy remains realistic and can be followed long-term. In addition, to expect a person to whip up a three-course meal like a Michelin star chef when they hate cooking is setting the path to failure. Fortunately, many nutrient-dense dishes do not require any cooking and certainly very little preparation time. When the bulk of any meal should include a variety of vegetables as per the government guideline of 5-a-day (that is the minimum of 5-a-day, not a negotiable number hovering below the number 5) then our challenge for Cherisse was to find a suitable variety of vegetables that can be enjoyed raw. The availability of already washed, cut, sliced, and diced options are such that you do not even need a cutting board and sharp kitchen knife for meal preparation anymore. As long as you have access to a supermarket, a plate and eating utensils you are set to go. Cherisse opted for vegetable juices because her energy needs are higher than average. This had the added advantage that she could have a liquid meal bursting with plant fibre (provided that she avoids the extraction method of juicing), vitamins, and minerals after a concert, late in the evening, when eating a solid meal could very well impact on her much-needed sleep because it requires more time to digest.

**Table 6**. Make your own juice

**Energy boost:** Carrot, spinach leaves, and mashed avocado, or
Lettuce leaves, stalks of celery, and tomatoes.

**Vitamin boost:** Carrots, spinach leaves, and beetroot

**Mineral boost:** Tomatoes, parsley, and turnip

*Add water or ice to dilute. You might initially choose to add an apple to sweeten your juice until you have acquired a taste for pure vegetable juices. To incorporate protein in these delicious juices, add a tablespoon of ground hemp or flaxseeds.*

For someone who needs to ensure that her energy levels support playing in a live concert with enthusiasm, zest, and exuberance, optimal nutrition, rest, and uninterrupted sleep are key. Like any top-level athlete the challenge is always to ensure that you can perform at your best at every sporting event or in Cherisse's case, stadium-filled performance.

Cherisse is not always on the road and when she is at home she enjoys making delicious meals, so for her, my simple health strategy could be incorporated both when travelling and when she was back at home. Less than a year after our initial meeting, Cherisse reported that her menstrual cycle and PMS symptoms had greatly improved despite her continued work commitments.

Five years since we first met, Cherisse continues to follow my simple rules in her daily life. Her workload has not eased, in fact, I believe it has increased, so when I approached her in 2017 to gain permission for inclusion in this book I was delighted to read her response:

"Good health and wellbeing are essential for being able to lead a full life. I developed asthma at a very early age and have found that keeping myself healthy has been vital to my life as a drummer. Being a touring musician means you have gruelling schedules and being a drummer is very physically demanding. Touring worldwide with various artists such as Mika, Paloma Faith, Bryan Ferry and now Simple Minds means that it is vital that I look after myself. I and the bands have calculated that I have been around the world more than 8 times – pretty mental! Having a healthy body and a healthy state of mind have contributed massively towards my ability to lead this high-energy working lifestyle. Because I play in a very physical way I find that after shows I am completely drained. I'd like to thank Wilma as I have found that eating the right foods and having a balanced diet has made all the difference to my state of mind and enjoyment of life!"

## Take-Home Message

- ➢ Stop smoking.
- ➢ Accept that you have a monthly menstrual cycle and that it can make you underperform for a few days per month, this is normal.
- ➢ Do not rely on medication to suppress your symptoms.
- ➢ Test your adrenal gland function via a salivary cortisol test.
- ➢ Test your thyroid function via a full thyroid blood screen.
- ➢ Exercise to combat stress and lose any excess weight.
- ➢ Introduce a great variety of legumes, nuts, and seeds into your diet.
- ➢ Strictly limit alcohol intake.
- ➢ Drink plenty of water.
- ➢ Ditch the milk chocolate, sweets, pastries, biscuits, and junk food and learn to prepare, eat, and enjoy nutritious, real food.

## Meal Ideas for Hormonal Balance

**Breakfast**

Porridge oats (made with water only) with 2 tablespoons of pumpkin seeds, sunflower seeds or ground flax seeds. Add ¼ cup of berries to sweeten (raspberries, blueberries, or strawberries)

**Lunch**

Lentil and vegetable soup with a slice of rye bread and avocado generously spread on top

**Dinner**

Stir fried vegetables (sugar snap peas, Chinese leaf, asparagus, shiitake mushrooms) with 125 g tofu

**Condiments**

Add a tablespoon of good quality olive oil to raw and cooked vegetables. Other options can include flaxseed, avocado, walnut and hempseed oils.

Refer to chapter 9 for a complete food list.

# Prepare Your Plate to Deal with Stress

## Stephen's Story

In 2010, Stephen contacted me because he needed help with stress-related insomnia and psoriasis.

*****

There are some people who can fill a room with an air of power, not the feeling you get when you are afraid of someone, rather the impression that before you stands a person who commands respect and at the same time is very approachable. Stephen is a 39-year-old married man and father of two. His jet-black hair is cut short and his chestnut-coloured eyes draw your attention. He is very soft spoken and I am grateful that my office is quiet enough for me not to have to ask him to raise his voice. I get the impression that Stephen rarely speaks loudly and that he nonetheless gets things done in his demanding job in the city of London. Stephen's work hours are not for the fainthearted and he tells me that his average working week hovers around the 65-hour mark. Those hours do not include being on call which can make his working week equate hours deemed hazardous under the European Commission's working time directive. I am shocked to hear that he can be called at any time of the night irrespective of whether it is a weekday or the weekend. This means that he can never completely switch off from his work demands nor can he know when he will be able to sleep through the night uninterrupted.

Stephen stands 182 cm (5 foot 10 inches) tall and weighs 78 kg (12 stone 3 pounds). He carries his weight well and his BMI equals 24, which is well within the normal range. He informs me that he has been suffering from insomnia for about 15 years and that his weight had suddenly increased by 13 kg (2 stone). That means that for most of his adult life, Stephen had a BMI of 19, which puts him at the other end of the normal weight spectrum. What strikes me are the very dark circles and bags under his eyes, and his eyebrows, or more accurately what few hairs are left, marred with the thick red skin associated with psoriasis, a chronic skin condition. It looks as if he is wearing a permanent eye mask given the area that the inflamed skin covers. He casually mentions that he had severely inflamed knee joints when he was at university where he was unable to walk without the use of crutches for about one year. Psoriasis is often associated with psoriatic arthritis or painful and swollen joints.

Here, we have a very hard-working businessman who finds himself in an environment where coffee, alcohol, rich food, and sometimes recreational drugs dominate. Not only do his extreme working hours place considerable demand on his time, he is also a committed family man with two dependent children. It seems that not one minute of his day is his own and even his sleep patterns are governed by work commitments. Can you imagine not being able to plan any time away from work because you are expected to be available at the drop of a hat? Most working people cope with their work commitments because at the end of a five-day week they can schedule two days of rest, relaxation or extramural activities. This type of working rhythm enables a person to recharge and regroup with regularity, whereas a person like Stephen is expected to remain switched on seven days a week without even a guaranteed uninterrupted night's sleep. This kind of lifestyle puts a great amount of stress on a person's body and if left unchanged can lead to serious health complications. The value of a good night's sleep, be it a continued period of 8 hours or less, is being flagged as imperative for long-term health outcomes. Sleep deprivation is said to increase the risk of cardiovascular disease, regardless of age, weight, smoking, and exercise habits. And ischaemic heart disease is still the leading cause of death for both men and women across the globe. This makes Stephen appear to be walking a tightrope or indeed being a ticking time bomb in terms of health outcome.

# The Impact of Stress

Let us have a look at what stress is and how it can affect your biology. Stress is defined as a state of mental or emotional strain or tension resulting from adverse or demanding circumstances. A stressful event can include moving house, getting married, planning a family, writing exams, changing employment, or even more subtly, trying to cope with the modern-day frenetic pace of life. Stress is also a biological term, which refers to the consequences suffered when your body fails to respond appropriately to emotional or physical stressors, such as bereavement or demanding physical exercise. The stress response can come into play whether the trigger is actual or indeed imagined. Whether you think you are stressed or not, if your physiology is showing symptoms of stress, then that is what is happening internally. To ignore symptoms of stress or 'just pushing through' can one day literally stop you in your tracks.

Picture yourself standing in line at a supermarket checkout till and the shopper in front of you is fumbling with his bags and then drops his wallet. He then needs to find his spectacles to locate the correct money only to realise that he does not have sufficient funds at hand. You, the next person in line, are in an incredible rush. You only have half an hour for lunch and you would like to eat your carefully selected food choice before you are needed back at your desk to continue your day, seated and very stationary until your next comfort break. As the person continues to complete his transaction at the speed of a resting sloth, you feel your blood pumping in your ears. You clench your teeth and you muster every thread of self-control not to punch something, or heaven forbid someone. You clearly find yourself in a state of stress.

**Table 7**. Common symptoms of stress
- Irritability, anxiety, tearfulness, low mood or depression Muscular tension and unexplained pain
- Inability to concentrate or worsening memory
- Headaches and migraines
- Accelerated heart rate and increased blood pressure Unexplained weight fluctuations

- Disrupted sleep such as insomnia
- Low libido

**Table 8**. Underlying causes of stress
- Difficult family life (conflict between family members)
- Unrealistic expectations and unachievable ambitions
- Social pressures
- Expectation of academic achievement and work success
- Dissatisfaction with your current situation or status
- Change in sleeping habits (shift work or travel)
- New responsibilities (marriage, dependent children, or ailing parents)
- Change in eating habits (dieting)
- Stress-prone diet (craving salt, caffeine, sugar, or alcohol)
- Change to a new environment (moving house or travelling)
- Money concerns

Let us look at how stress can affect your physiology, that is, the many intricate inner workings of your body. Virtually, any stressful event triggers an array of neural and biochemical reactions that prepare your body to cope with the consequences of that event. The immediate reaction to a stressful situation is the release of the major stress hormones, adrenaline (epinephrine) and noradrenaline (norepinephrine) from the adrenal glands situated on top of your kidneys at the back of your body. These two hormones start a cascade of events, including an increased heart rate, to circulate blood throughout the body, specifically reaching the arms and legs to allow you to either fight or flee. We may live in the modern world free of predatory animals roaming the street, however, your genetic make-up is programmed to deal with any stress event just like your primitive forefathers did. A little-known fact is that digestive function grinds to a halt when you are in the midst of a stress event because you do not have much reason to process a meal when you are either fighting or fleeing an opponent threatening your life. Once the initial stress reaction is set in motion the brain joins the activity and sends out messengers to further accommodate all the biological changes that are needed in this ongoing, energy-demanding battle.

Other organs are jolted into action and a complex succession of chain reactions is set in motion. The cost of an ongoing stress response can include an acceleration of the ageing process by forcing organs to work harder over a shorter period of time *and* hinder the much-needed growth and repair processes to allow for damage control incurred via every stress event. Remember that if your body is pouring all its energy into helping you cope with a stress event, very little is available to maintain the other much-needed functions that require energy to be completed. Prolonged stress is detrimental to the cardiovascular system as it results in considerable wear and tear of the blood vessels due to the heart having to work so hard to help you cope. The organ responsible for getting blood to your extremities is the heart, which at that moment has to work harder than normal to pump nutrients where they are most needed. Keep in mind that your blood not only transports a host of protective cells to any site of damage, like a cut or a bruise, it also transports nutrients around our whole system, reaching the hair on our heads and everywhere in between all the way down to the tip of our toes.

Another major side-effect of an ongoing stress response is that it can lower your immune status. You might have experienced times where your fall ill as soon as you take time off work to go on holiday. Whilst you are in that stress event, being obliged to be at the office every day, your defence system is working overtime, but as soon as you leave all that imaginary fighting and fleeing behind, your body realises that it is running low on defence strategies and you get the inevitable cold or flu. Additionally, when we shift our focus to the gut, the epicentre of the digestive process, prolonged stress diminishes your good gut bacteria and as a consequence allows the bad bacteria to multiply beyond safe numbers. This is one of the pivotal reasons why people who are stressed often experience symptoms consistent with IBS. You might be one of those people who gain weight during a stressful period, not because you necessarily eat more, but because your digestion is no longer working optimally and your food finds a permanent resting place around your abdomen. Stress can enhance the taste of certain foods especially those which are overwhelmingly fatty and sugary. This drive for non-essential food options can trip up even the most motivated amongst us. Not only are you figuratively speaking tearing your hair out during a stress event, your willpower is scattered in the wind.

When someone approaches me with IBS symptoms I can often draw a link to a stressful event in that person's life such as a recent separation, moving home, miscarriage, redundancy, public speaking events, exams, changing school or going to university, and travels abroad where you are more likely to suffer from traveller's diarrhoea. Due to the negative effect of stress on our anatomy and physiology, we see that prolonged episodes require a higher level of nutritional support to help our bodies repair. Given the nutritional shortfall of the modern standard American and British diet and our frenetic pace of life, it is no small wonder that an increasing amount of people walk into my clinic and ask my help with stress-related symptoms, just as Stephen did.

When it comes to food choices, let us see what Stephen's diet looked like when he first approached me. The ideal plate composition, in contrast, consist of ½ **V**egetables, ¼ **P**rotein, and ¼ **C**arbohydrates

■ Protein　　　■ Vegetables　　　■ Carbohydrates

Stephen's Plate Composition

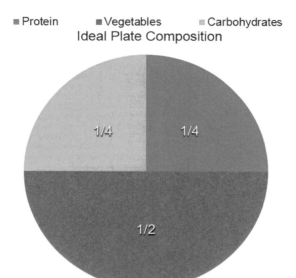

At first glance, it can seem that Stephen has an exemplary diet, with an abundance of vegetables and the ideal ratio of carbohydrates. However, if we investigate further we see that he is significantly under consuming important protein food options. The first concern is that Stephen's growth and repair systems are already impaired due to his erratic sleep/ wake cycle. The dark circles and bags under his eyes show that he is not regenerating healthy cells to replace the damaged ones, and his ongoing psoriasis is further testament to the fact that this family man needs to address this deficiency if he is to continue to fulfil his demanding role as the sole breadwinner.

## Protein, the Full Story

When people mention the word protein, the most obvious image that springs to mind is a barbecue where the offerings overwhelmingly include large beef steaks, hot dogs, and hamburger patties. And in terms of diet, you might instantly think of the Atkins or Banting diet or more recently the Palaeolithic diet. People are shying away from these diets because they are linked with an increase in cardiovascular disease and stroke risk. The problem with these controversial diets is not related to the protein content per se, rather with the lack of vegetables in the diet. To dispel the myths associated with protein, let us explore the nutritional value and look at foods which contain protein in line with a healthy outcome.

Protein consumption is paramount in human nutrition because it is required to manufacture the structural components of muscle tissue, enzymes, haemoglobin, antibodies, hormones, and transport proteins. Without adequate protein intake you could risk the following:

- muscle wasting or diminished muscle mass termed cachexia in the medical literature,
- digestive enzyme under secretion, which can lead to symptoms of indigestion or heartburn,
- the diminished capability of the red blood cells to efficiently carry oxygen around the body,
- the inability to fight off infections,
- hormone associated illnesses such as under or overactive thyroid function, and
- cellular malfunction due to the inability of specific transport proteins to move certain molecules within a cell or from the inside to the outside of the cell and vice versa.

**Table 9**. Signs of possible protein deficiency (which includes malabsorption)

| | |
|---|---|
| Energy: | Experiencing constant or recurring fatigue even when little physical or mental activity was undertaken |
| Mood: | Low mood and depression not associated with periods of grief or significant emotional events |
| Hair: | Unhealthy looking hair, whether thinning, loss of, dry, coarse, or brittle |
| Mouth: | Noticeable gum recession and bleeding |
| Nails: | Vertical corrugations (beaded nails), pronounced central ridge, horizontal grooves, splitting, soft, thickened |

| | |
|---|---|
| Muscles: | Atrophy (wasting), losing muscle mass without dieting, or weakness even without embarking on intense physical activity |
| Skin: | Easily bruised and slow to heal after cuts and scrapes |
| Growth: | Slow or poor growth when compared to peers |
| Legs: | Visibly swollen (oedema) or painful legs |

If any of the above symptoms pertain to you, take a look at the amount and choices of protein that you eat. If your diet is in line with the ideal plate composition, please ensure that you ask your doctor to investigate further.

Your body not only needs protein, it also needs a sufficient quantity of each of the amino acids, the building blocks of protein. Imagine protein being a Lego® house, strong, aesthetically pleasing, and the cornerstone of your Lego® village. Amino acids are the individual Lego® blocks in different shapes and sizes each slotting neatly into a specific gap. There are 20 amino acids in total, of which 9 are essential. Essential meaning that without eating foods that contain these 9 amino acids your body will be deficient, lacking, and unable to manufacture it. Our bodies have many mechanisms enabling it to make nutrients from other nutrients. When you hear the word essential pertaining to nutrition, it means that you have to eat those particular nutrients as the body is unable to derive it from another nutrient. For example, a diesel car cannot function optimally on petrol and many people have had to telephone a motoring association because they have absentmindedly inserted the wrong nozzle in their vehicle's fuel tank. These days engineers are designing the nozzles with different circumferences to make it impossible to insert a petrol pump nozzle into a diesel car's fuel tank input opening. Nature has not developed such an obvious solution yet, however, it does let you know that something is amiss via presenting symptoms. The fact that many people ignore those warning signs or even consider them normal, results in illnesses becoming very severe over time and requiring medical intervention, such as developing type II diabetes because the pancreas has altered its function over time in part due to ill-advised food choices.

**Table 10**. The essential role of protein in the human body
- Strength
- Building and maintaining muscle tissue
- Maintaining immune function
- Recovery from injury
- Growth and development
- Balancing blood glucose levels

Every committed bodybuilder will wax lyrical about their developing muscle tissue and will fastidiously exercise and eat in such a way as to increase and define their muscles. For those who are not bodybuilders, who mainly focus on muscle definition for aesthetic value, muscles have very important functions. They are primarily responsible for the movement of the human body. Without proper muscle development, patients develop ataxia (balance and coordination difficulties). This movement includes walking, shaking your head, staying upright in a chair, your heart beating, assisting circulation, and peristalsis in the gut to support regular bowel movements.

## The Role and Function of Protein in the Human Body

Other than the structural role that protein plays it is important to take a deeper look into your biology to understand the importance of protein molecules. The inner working of our biology is complex and when you read warnings pertaining to high protein dietary intake you might be concerned that eating too much protein can have a detrimental effect. To understand the importance of ensuring that ¼ of your meals consist of protein dense food choices, we take a look at the various parts of your anatomy and physiology that are made up of protein molecules and are essential for optimal bodily function. These parts of your biological make-up require a steady supply of dietary protein to ensure that they can perform optimally and regenerate when depleted. Without them, your health status is compromised.

# Enzymes

Enzymes play their part in speeding up biological reactions in the body. They behave a little like the Pied Piper of Hamelin who led the rats quickly and in an ordered fashion out of town with his musical talent. Enzymes consist of a protein part and a cofactor or helper molecule, which is often a micronutrient like magnesium or calcium. Enzymes in the body help digestion, breaking down food particles to more manageable sizes, transform glucose into usable energy, and copy your genetic information or blueprint in the form of deoxyribonucleic acid (DNA) to allow for new cells and tissue to form. This is a major function because, unbeknownst to you, every time you use an organ it needs to be patched and repaired to restore itself to its former undamaged state. The action of repair is not only required when you cut, bump, or are involved in a traumatic physical event. Reparation in our bodies is a 24-hour, non-stop event.

# Haemoglobin

Haemoglobin is the transport system in your body that ensures that all the organs, however far from the heart, receive oxygen.

# Antibodies

Antibodies make up your defence system, that crucial part of you that protects you from constant danger. Your skin covers your body and once something pierces that barrier, be it a knife wound or a scratch, your antibodies line up to ensure that whatever micro-organism you are exposed to at that moment, is neutralised or destroyed. Our unique biological design gifted us with a few orifices, i.e. openings such as nostrils, a mouth, anus, and those in the genital area. These open areas are also guarded by antibodies that control the immediate environment in such a way that it discourages foreign organisms from finding it too comfortable to set up permanent residence. Patients who are immunocompromised, meaning they have a glitch in their antibody production or function, lack one or more part of the normal defence hierarchy. If part of the protective mechanism is dysfunctional, the individual is at a higher risk of ill-health and will recover more slowly. That is why the human immunodeficiency virus (HIV) positive patients are at high risk of becoming ill compared to a non-affected person. Their fighting army's budget has been severely cut and no longer offers even basic protection. The risk of death from non-HIV related factors is greatly increased due to this physiological protection malfunction. For immunocompromised patients, it is especially important that their diet and lifestyle supply optimal health support because their biology is not working as well as it could.

## Hormones

Hormones range from sex to stress hormones and form an integral part of how your body and mind behave. Progesterone, an important female sex hormone, prepares and enables successful pregnancy. Oxytocin aids the birthing process and once the infant is born, prolactin acts on the mammary glands to enable mothers to breastfeed. Human Growth Hormone (HGH) is responsible for growth spurts in children and adolescents and helps regulate your sugar and fat metabolism (the breakdown of carbohydrate and fats in the diet to usable energy in the body). Thyroid-stimulating hormone (TSH) is responsible for the secretion of the thyroid hormones, triiodothyronine (T3) and thyroxine (T4) that maintain metabolic function. Your body depends on optimal thyroid hormone secretion for temperature control, the breakdown of fats, reducing levels of cholesterol in the blood, growth, and development of the nervous system.

The stress hormone, cortisol, plays an integral part in breaking down amino acids needed to make enzymes, energy production, the breakdown of triglycerides, immune depression, and to dampen inflammation. Insulin ensures that increased blood glucose levels are reduced to acceptable levels needed for optimal function. Melatonin, secreted at night-time, enables you to have a good night's sleep, thereby setting your body's biological clock and allowing you to recover from the day's activities.

Gastrin, found in the stomach, ensures that enough gastric juices are secreted to help you digest your food and enable the components of your meal to move from the stomach to the small intestine. Secretin and cholecystokinin continue the process of digestion in the small intestine, there where nutrients are extracted from the food we eat. Leptin, found in your fat cells (adipose tissue) signal that you have had enough to eat.

Your heart is also affected by hormones. Atrial natriuretic peptide is responsible for lowering blood pressure, a vital role given that high blood pressure is a serious cardiovascular disease risk.

The athletic world is constantly rocked by news of athletes doping, which means they are taking hormonal substances which are believed to better athletic performance. Men have higher testosterone (one of the sex hormones) than women and that is what makes them behave and look like men, i.e. be more muscular, aggressive, and have higher sex drives, compared to the average woman. When a woman artificially increases her testosterone levels, her athletic performance can be bettered and result in physical (becoming more muscular) and mental (aggression) changes. These are viewed as unfair advantages in sport.

To ensure that your hormonal secretion is adequate when required, your body will need a steady supply of protein molecules that is secured when you eat protein dense food at all meals.

## Neurotransmitters

In the central nervous system, we find several amino acids that are classified as neurotransmitters. Their role is to enhance communication via the synapses or alternatively inhibit transmission of messages. These include glutamate (glutamic acid), aspartate (aspartic acid), gamma-aminobutyric acid (GABA), and glycine. GABA makes up approximately one-third of all brain synapses.

## Cells and Organelles

Every inch of your body is made up of cells. These cells contain different organelles, each with a different function. A bit like a beehive where every type of bee has its own role to play and these roles do not overlap. In order for this intricate system to work, nutrients are moved from the inside of the cell to the outside, and vice versa. Transport or carrier proteins facilitate this function. They are embedded in the cell membrane and act like gatekeepers and the postal system, all in one. Without them, essential nutrients cannot enter or exit a cell and that results in reduced efficiency and ultimately leads to a deficiency of certain elements and accumulation of waste products in the cell.

For example, in diabetes, the health risk is because glucose, the body's preferred energy source, is not pulled back into the cell to be stored for future use, due to a lack of insulin (a hormone secreted by the pancreas). This results in elevated blood glucose levels (hyperglycaemia), hugely detrimental to overall physiology because it damages the blood vessels. Excess glucose in the bloodstream requires insulin to normalise the circulating levels. When your eating preferences include options that convert to glucose easily (refined carbohydrates and sugary drinks) and you lead an inactive lifestyle, your pancreas will be required to release insulin frequently. Prolonged periods of this cycle – high blood glucose requiring insulin response – can lead to insulin resistance and ultimately increase your chances of developing type II diabetes.

A good supply of glucose is imperative for physical activity such as exercise. However, when you are sedentary, such as working in an office setting where you sit for most of your day or drive a heavy goods vehicle from country to country, excess glucose, gained from food, is destined to be stored in the adipose (fat) tissue. Repeat this scenario over and over and the end result is an expanding waist and an increase in body mass edging towards a state of overweight or worse, obesity, a global health concern given its association with cardiovascular disease.

Protein molecules, supplied by dietary intake of protein dense food, ensure that cells have the building blocks to regenerate when they are needed. Given that your body is constructed of trillions of individual cells which need constant replacing, your need for protein-rich food is an undeniable fact.

# The Role of Dietary Protein

**Table 11**. Signs of poor blood glucose control

- Craving for sweets
- Poor memory and/or concentration
- Craving for stimulants (tea, coffee, or cigarettes)
- Thoughts less focused, fuzzier
- Headaches
- Fatigue or weakness if a meal is missed
- Often feeling agitated, easily upset or nervous
- Irritability or mood swings if a meal is missed
- Occasional shakiness, jitteriness or tremors
- Feelings of confusion or disorientation
- Awaken from sleep feeling tired or restless

An important point to clarify is the belief that certain grains, like quinoa, are high protein sources. Yes, quinoa does contain more protein when compared to brown rice but is not superior when compared to a pure protein like boiled eggs or indeed hempseed.

**Table 12**. Protein content of various grain products per 100 g

| Food | Protein per 100 g (g) | Carbohydrate per 100 g (g) | Carbohydrate/protein ratio |
|------|------|------|------|
| Boiled egg (a high protein option for comparison) | 13 | 1 | 0.08 |
| Hempseed (a vegan high protein option for comparison) | 34.5 | 1.1 | 0.03 |
| Amaranth | 4 | 19 | 4.8 |
| Basmati rice | 9 | 76.2 | 8.5 |
| Brown rice | 3 | 23 | 7.7 |
| Buckwheat | 13 | 71 | 5.5 |
| Bulgar wheat* | 14.8 | 72.2 | 4.9 |
| Oats | 3 | 11 | 3.7 |
| Polenta | 7.4 | 76.8 | 8.5 |
| Pop corn (plain) | 9.4 | 67 | 7.1 |
| Quinoa* | 14 | 64 | 4.8 |
| Sweetcorn | 2.4 | 11.8 | 4.9 |
| White maize | 6.6 | 74 | 11.2 |
| White rice | 2 | 21 | 10.5 |
| White rice pasta | 3 | 21 | 7 |

The number comparison in the table above shows that when you enjoy quinoa in a meal you are simultaneously eating almost five times more carbohydrates, which translates into a deficit in terms of protein when aiming to achieve the ideal plate composition. Conversely, when you add hempseed to your meal, you can add a similar quantity of any starch option because hempseed supply almost no carbohydrates. These very important facts around blood glucose control and weight concerns, with regards to protein, are what drive people to follow low carbohydrate diets such as the Palaeolithic, Atkins, and Specific Carbohydrate Diet.

## Protein Food Options

Protein dense food options include land and water animal flesh, eggs, nuts, seeds, and legumes. Note, yet again, that with the exception of tofu and hempseed, all other plant-derived protein options (nuts, seeds, and legumes) come complete with a helping of carbohydrates, and are not pure protein foods. If you decide that a lentil soup is your meal choice go easy on the starch additions such as potatoes, croutons, and bread because lentils already contain a substantial amount of carbohydrates. Red lentils, for example, contain more than double the amount of carbohydrates compared to protein and sunflower seeds have almost equal amounts of both these important macronutrients. Many grains, fruit, and vegetables contain some protein but are not a major dietary protein contributor. People who follow a vegetarian or stricter vegan diet have chosen to eliminate animal flesh (meat and fish) and animal derivatives (eggs and dairy, such as cheese, yoghurt, and milk) from their daily diet. If you are vegetarian or indeed vegan you should be aware that by choosing to eliminate an easily accessible source of protein you need to be extra vigilant by including plant-based protein such as tofu, legumes, nuts, and seeds. If you neglect to replace animal protein with other comparable plant-based alternatives your body will be supplied with a source of energy (provided that you do not neglect to eat), but you will risk missing out on an essential macronutrient. Energy from non-protein dense food allows you to meet your daily energy needs, however, without eating adequate amounts of protein your body may struggle to stimulate growth and development and support a host of other necessary biological tasks. Being a healthy vegetarian or strict vegan is easy, just make sure that you too follow the ideal plate composition ratios.

**Table 9.** A list of protein-rich foods highlighting the protein and carbohydrate content

| Food | Protein per 100 g (g) | Carbohydrate per 100 g (g) |
|---|---|---|
| Chickpeas | 7.7 | 17.4 |
| Haricot beans | 6.6 | 17.2 |
| Red kidney beans | 8.4 | 17.4 |
| Aduki beans | 9.3 | 22.5 |
| Mung beans | 7.6 | 15.3 |
| Butter beans | 5.9 | 13.0 |
| Red lentils | 23.8 | 56.0 |
| Tofu | 8.1 | 0.7 |
| Walnuts | 14.7 | 3.3 |
| Almonds | 21.1 | 6.9 |
| Brazil nuts | 6.5 | 1.4 |
| Cashew nuts | 17.7 | 18.1 |
| Hazelnuts | 14.1 | 6.0 |
| Pumpkin seeds | 24.4 | 15.2 |
| Sunflower seeds | 19.8 | 18.6 |
| Linseeds (flaxseeds) | 22.1 | 3.0 |
| Sesame seeds | 18.2 | 0.9 |
| Hempseeds | 34.5 | 1.1 |

| Food | Protein per 100 g (g) | Carbohydrate per 100 g (g) |
|---|---|---|
| Salmon (grilled) | 24.2 | 0 |
| Trout (grilled) | 21.5 | 0 |
| Halibut (grilled) | 25.3 | 0 |
| Mackerel (grilled) | 19.1 | 0 |
| Sardines (grilled) | 23.3 | 0 |
| Herring (grilled) | 13.7 | 0 |
| Tuna (canned) | 23.5 | 0 |
| Eggs (chicken) | 12.5 | 0 |
| Eggs (ducks) | 14.6 | 0 |
| Turkey | 20.1 | 0 |
| Chicken | 27.3 | 0 |
| Pheasant | 14.5 | 0 |
| Duck | 25.3 | 0 |
| Lamb | 15.4 | 0 |
| Beef (sirloin steak) | 26.4 | 0 |
| Pork | 26.1 | 0 |
| Venison | 22.2 | 0 |

Data source: *McCance & Widdowson*

Stephen's diet is lacking in protein necessary to support him during his continuous exposure to work stress. He does not need to (figuratively speaking) start hunting every available animal or animal-derived product to meet his protein needs. Apart from ethical and sustainability arguments, the experts in the field of human nutrition caution against overconsumption of animal products, which includes meat, poultry, fish, eggs, and dairy products such as milk, cheese, and yoghurt. Diseases such as cardiovascular disease, diabetes, and cancer have been linked with consumption of animal products. Given that Stephen is already a strong candidate for cardiovascular ill health, he should choose plant-based protein options to replenish his protein needs.

Many people follow a strict vegetarian diet guided by religious and moral beliefs. This shows that we do not need to consume animal-based products to ensure adequate protein intake. So, to optimise his long-term health goals, Stephen is encouraged to implement healthy food choices and to develop a positive taste relationship with the bountiful plant-based food options so abundantly grown in nature. Given that he follows an inclusive (omnivore) diet, it is imperative that he chooses sustainable, ethically sourced options and continues to balance it with ample vegetables (at the same meal). This crucial combination ensures that his gut function is supported both in terms of encouraging beneficial bacteria to thrive and preventing constipation or sluggish bowel movements, which are risk factors for bowel cancers.

Given that Stephen gets so little sleep most nights it is not unusual for him to reach for a caffeine kick first thing in the morning and during the day when he feels that his attention is waning. Fortunately, he does not indulge in the more commonly ordered calorific cappuccino or latte versions with added sugar or sweetener. Stephen's caffeine beverage of choice is a strong espresso with nothing added, just a strong, black, caffeine hit. This is also his breakfast of choice. No croissant, buttered toast, cereal, bacon butty or full English fry-up, just a black, bitter, cup of coffee.

## Caffeine, Friend or Foe?

If you are to believe media coverage there is no end to the health properties of coffee. Unfortunately, the message changes almost daily and it explains why people can be left more confused than adequately informed. To understand the origins of this humble bean, let us have a look at the history of one of the most produced hot beverages. According to the National Geographic magazine, coffee has its origins in Ethiopia where around 800 AD Kaldi, a goatherd, noted his flock grazing on the cherry-red berries of a coffee shrub. They seemed to dance from one shrub to another and he decided to nibble on the berries as well. Soon he was dancing with the animals. Witnessing Kaldi's goatly gambol, a monk gathered berries for his brothers and that evening they were uncannily alert to divine inspiration. History indicates that other Africans of that era used to fuel up on protein-rich coffee-and-animal-fat balls, probably the first energy snack enjoyed by man.

Modern-day coffee started its journey in Arabia where beans were roasted and brewed around 1000 AD. By the 13th century, Muslims were drinking coffee regularly and wherever the Islamic faith went, coffee was taken too. North Africa, the eastern Mediterranean and India soon adopted coffee drinking ritualistically. Europe benefited from the coffee bean around 1615 where the Dutch, initially, were the most successful in cultivating the bean. It took many years before the humble coffee bean established in South America and by the 1800s, Brazilians were harvesting mass amounts, which turned coffee from an elite indulgence to an everyday elixir, a drink for the people. These days there is no end to the myriad of coffee outlets marketing this wonder bean.

The National Coffee Association of U.S.A. published a fact sheet highlighting the health benefits of coffee. They stipulate that coffee:

- ✓ Has more fibre than orange juice, and antioxidants too,
- ✓ Keeps your mouth moist,
- ✓ Can improve handwriting,
- ✓ Wakes you up,
- ✓ Does not make you shaky, and
- ✓ Can improve your mood.

Caffeine is a socially acceptable drug that is widely consumed throughout the world. Not to be viewed quite in the same way as snake oil but do not be fooled into thinking that the coffee bean is a superfood or that its effect on the human body is innocuous. The effects of caffeine are noticeable on the nervous system such that many people know when they have had too many cups in a given day. Drinking coffee and other caffeine-containing drinks can cause your heart to beat faster, make you more alert and even affect the dilation of your pupils. These responses are akin to the fight or flight response associated with stress. Remember that this results in your liver releasing more glucose into the bloodstream to raise your blood sugar levels and digestive function is significantly reduced or even completely shut down. As previously mentioned, this kind of response can result in drastic changes in the gut bacteria which is associated with ill health. Even though immediate effects may differ greatly from person to person, the long-term effect is not deemed beneficial for a vast majority of the population. Perhaps this is why no health agency promotes the use of coffee for health benefits when dealing with infants, children or even young adults.

Some individuals are less sensitive to these responses whereas many others find that caffeine causes a myriad of undesirable side-effects such as:

- muscle twitching,
- anxiety,
- increased blood pressure,
- irregular heartbeat,
- digestive complaints,
- headaches,
- erratic sleeping patterns.

Of course you, like Stephen, might be one of those people who simply ignore these warning signs because coffee is an integral part of your lifestyle. Given the conflicting reports that make the headlines, it is no surprise that many people simply shrug and think that the negative reports are the work of health zealots.

In the world of professional sport, caffeine is an accepted component of many athletes' diet and although it has no nutritional value, coffee and caffeine products are commonly used to improve sports performance. This is due to research suggesting the caffeine intake improves time to exhaustion and work output during endurance exercise. In layman's terms, that means that caffeine can help you exercise longer before you feel tired. Using a cup of coffee to wake you up for those early race starts certainly has merit if you are normally a late riser. The downside, however, is that over-consumption may result in gastric upset and poor hydration status, despite what the National Coffee Association fact sheet would have us believe. Caffeine is a naturally occurring diuretic that inhibits sodium reabsorption and results in slower re-uptake of water by the kidneys. Simply put, that means that despite you drinking a cup of liquid, depending on your measure of choice ranging from an espresso cup to a large mug, you are more likely to lose fluid.

Caffeine is not only an irritant in the digestive tract causing acid reflux, heartburn, or diarrhoea, it also stimulates the kidneys to help you urinate more frequently or indeed in greater volume. This physiological state of dehydration can accentuate signs of early ageing, wrinkled or sagging skin, and hinder your athletic performance in the long run. Urine is an excellent way for the body to release unwanted waste products. Remember that in terms of human health outcomes, waste products are always best excreted than left to circulate in the body. But if you are continuously causing your kidneys to produce and release urine, you are at greater risk of becoming dehydrated and losing water-soluble vitamins and critical electrolytes, including calcium, sodium (salt), potassium, and magnesium. Losing these minerals via urinary excretion when your diet is already sub-optimal can severely affect your health.

In the world of professional sports, the World Anti Doping Agency (WADA) decided to remove caffeine from the list of prohibited substances in 2004. They considered caffeine to be a weak stimulant with limited performance-enhancing effect. It is also difficult to distinguish between normal use and the athlete's attempt to misuse. Even though caffeine no longer is a banned substance it is still monitored by WADA. Before you think that five or more cups of Java per day is nothing worth worrying about, remember that it used to be a banned substance, albeit for professional athletes only.

The science states that for the general population a moderate amount of coffee is equivalent to that contained in two cups of coffee on any given day. Individuals who experience side-effects associated with the ingestion of coffee are advised to abstain from all products containing caffeine, which can include coffee, hot chocolate, energy drinks, and chocolate. At one end of the spectrum, some animal studies have suggested that there is a possible link between caffeine intake and birth defects. This has resulted in the United States Food and Drug Administration recommending that expectant mothers avoid or greatly reduce intake during pregnancy. Fortunately, at the other end of the spectrum, there appears to be some benefit in drinking some coffee, some of the time. Nutritionally speaking a cup of black coffee has zero value, meaning it contains no nutrients that are deemed *essential* for long-term health. When coffee is used as a meal replacement, not only is there no nutritional gain, many physiological pathways may be disrupted.

Breakfast choices that include coffee combined with refined carbohydrate products that are calorie dense and nutrient deplete may be a contributing factor in the increasing incidence of ill health. Many people deem a latte and a muffin as the ultimate, standard breakfast choice. Think about that combination for a minute when compared to the ideal plate composition.

Here is a graph based on a Starbucks™ 2% milk, Venti latte combined with a blueberry muffin with yoghurt and honey

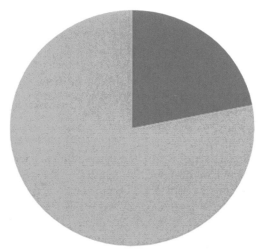

■ Protein        ■ Vegetables        ▪ Carbohydrates
**Latte and Blueberry Muffin Composition**

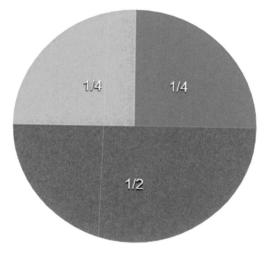

You might be thinking that this graph is not that bad when compared to the ideal plate composition given that the protein ratio is almost spot on. The protein from this meal comes from milk, egg, soya in the muffin, and milk in the latte. Remember that the experts in human nutrition caution against overconsumption of animal products, which include eggs and dairy products. This standard breakfast option seems to get almost all of the protein content from those two options. This is acceptable when you have this kind of breakfast occasionally, but too many people exclusively enjoy this meal at the start of every day of their working week. Look around you when it is snack time, many people opt for this combination of a large milky coffee and a pastry then *as well*. Not only are we starting the day with a powerful sugar and caffeine hit, many people are opting for another one or more servings throughout the day, not counting their lunch and dinner meal options. When you add up what a person eats in a day the empty calories are noticeable. There is no evidence that this meal option is conducive to long-term health never mind ideal weight management. If you are still indulging in this kind of breakfast or indeed choosing it as a morning or mid-afternoon snack, now is the time to consider better food options to attain your health goals.

Some people may enjoy coffee purely for the taste and choose to have a cup a day or two once in a while. They do not get coffee 'cravings' and do not need caffeine as a 'pick me up' or 'help me stay awake'. For these select members of the human race, caffeine may be harmless and pose no ill effects. However, knowing that coffee beans are mass produced in countries where there may be no strict herbicide and pesticide plantation regulations, you might want to consider the long-term health implications of consuming something that offers no direct nutritional value in the case of an espresso and excess empty calories when opting for a latte and muffin combination. Healthier herbal tea alternatives are plentiful and Stephen decided to include these instead of coffee every day after midday. He found that he quite enjoys chamomile and mint teas and still manages to stay alert. This is an important step towards helping him to start addressing his insomnia. Yes, we cannot change the fact that he is on call so often, however, it is imperative to help him sleep better at least on the nights when he is not called to work.

## What Happened to Stephen?

Stephen slowly incorporated the suggested dietary changes paying particular attention to the amount and kinds of proteins that he chose to include on a daily basis. He found that he absolutely loves legumes in the form of lentils and chickpeas, and opted for more fish such as mackerel as opposed to a man-sized steak. He tells me that his favourite meal is grilled fish with a large mixed salad liberally dressed with extra virgin olive oil. He still enjoys his espresso first thing in the morning but come midday, he chooses herbal teas or water to keep him hydrated. He has also started to eat a combination of nuts and fresh fruit for breakfast.

When it comes to skin health, there is an irrefutable link between skin conditions, including acne, eczema, and psoriasis and gut microbes – the undesirable ones. In Stephen's case, we uncovered a significant bacterial infection via a non-invasive comprehensive stool analysis. Surprisingly enough that same test revealed that Stephen has an excellent beneficial profile despite not taking any probiotic supplements or regularly eating yoghurt. This is an interesting finding given his stressful lifestyle.

Despite Stephen's work obligations continuing to put extreme pressure on his time, his psoriasis has completely healed, his joints no longer ache, and with regular sun exposure, the dark circles under his eyes have greatly diminished.

When I contacted him in 2017, he said the following:

"I went to see Wilma because a colleague strongly recommended I go see her. I was not expecting much as I thought I knew it all. I knew that my lifestyle was not ideal but I knew what needed to be done to support me through it; I knew about good nutrition. I knew about the importance of exercise and relaxation and was proficient in yoga and meditation techniques. I knew about the importance of good sleep. I doubted there was much that could be done for me without a drastic change in circumstances. It turns out I didn't quite know everything. The consultation with Wilma was thorough and professional, and although we did agree to pursue testing to get a more complete understanding of what was happening to me physiologically, I was surprised to hear that my food choices could improve. I scored high marks on carbs, but my ratio of vegetables to proteins was all wrong. Although I wasn't entirely convinced, Wilma's professionalism and reliance on facts rather than misguided wishful thinking often seen in alternative health practitioners convinced me to try altering my diet. I am so glad I did. Apart from the unexpected side effect of enjoying my meals even more, my quality of sleep is now far better than it has ever been. I fall asleep more easily, sleep longer, and feel more rested. Considering little else has changed in my lifestyle, I can only attribute this to the changes I made under Wilma's guidance. I am truly grateful I had the opportunity to see her."

## Take-Home Message

> ➤ Stop smoking.
> ➤ Coffee is not the long-term solution to impaired sleep patterns.
> ➤ Alcohol does not fix any problems.
> ➤ Protein is an essential nutrient and should be part of *all* your meals.
> ➤ Stress affects your gut bacteria. A comprehensive stool analysis requiring multiple samples will show how extensive and protective your microbiota is.
> ➤ If you cannot change your lifestyle, changing your diet is key.

## Meal Ideas to Balance Blood Glucose

### Breakfast
2 Egg omelette (no dairy added) with red bell pepper, tomatoes, kale. Add fresh cress and basil once cooked

### Lunch
Fish sushi with miso soup and carrot or beetroot juice

### Dinner
125 g grilled mackerel with broccoli, sweetcorn, fennel and spinach

### Condiments
Add a tablespoon of good quality olive oil to raw and cooked vegetables. Other options can include flaxseed, walnut, avocado, and hempseed oils.

Refer to chapter 9 for a complete food list.

# Prepare Your Plate to Address Eczema

## Maya's Story

Maya, a vivacious, blond-haired, blue-eyed girl has just turned 9 when we meet. She has a vibrant personality and is the eldest of three children. Photographs of her as an infant show a tiny bundle of joy with a red rash from the top of her head to the tip of her toes. At four months of age, her head was covered in cradle cap, a common occurrence for many infants.

\*\*\*\*\*

Maya's start in life was textbook perfect. She was conceived naturally, her mother followed an exemplary diet and avoided alcohol, tobacco smoke, coffee, and medication throughout her pregnancy. Born at 41 weeks via natural delivery, Maya was breastfed for a period of 10 months. The research linking natural birth and breastfeeding with optimal gut microbiota is overwhelming. Maya started her journey to solid food in the form of apple and carrots at 8 months and the introduction of standard infant formula only occurred at 13 months. Mum reports that Maya's skin rash is linked to an adverse reaction to one of the standard immunisation protocols. This never subsided despite her consultant paediatrician prescribing medication in the form of a standard penicillin and antibiotic combination for this type of skin affliction.

Maya has a good appetite, in fact, her mother states that it is perhaps a little too good. The whole family follows a diet which mum makes from scratch at home with an excellent range of ingredients like quinoa, buckwheat, barley, chickpeas, red meat, duck, fish, and a vast array of different vegetables. Maya's mother is so focused on good nutrition that she even makes her own stock, sauces, and fermented kefir. It is safe to say that this family chooses food that surpasses the average UK family's choices, and yet, here we have a little girl whose skin is severely affected despite no obvious genetic link.

Let us have a look at Maya's plate composition.

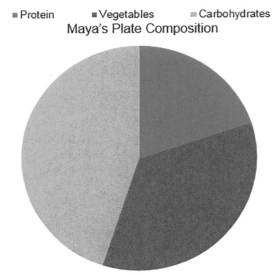

Maya's food choices, at first glance, look very healthy. Let us familiarise ourselves again with the ideal plate composition for comparison.

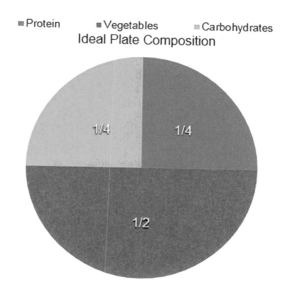

Ideal Plate Composition

- Protein
- Vegetables
- Carbohydrates

## Nutrition for Children

You might be thinking that children need a different plate composition, perhaps more focused on carbohydrate content given their continuous development. History shows us that children have often suffered from malnutrition. This was due to the scarcity of food and large families, where 2.2 children were the exception rather than the modern-day norm. Many households tell tales of 10 or more siblings as recent as a few decades ago. The lifestyle associated with larger families was often linked with demanding physical work environments such as farming. Food was in short supply and the dietary needs of the older, more physically able adults were placed before that of the younger members of the family. Fast forward to today and we see a significant reduction in physical activity and the increased availability of food. The incidence of obesity is not exclusively an adult population phenomenon. Childhood obesity is becoming a worldwide concern. The WHO report from October 2014 state that the number of overweight or obese children (aged between 0 and 5 years) has increased from 32 million (1990) to 42 million (2013) globally. The projection is that these numbers will increase to 70 million (2025) if the same trend continues.

Children instinctively tend to eat smaller quantities than adults and this plate composition of ½ **V**egetables, ¼ **P**rotein, and ¼ **C**arbohydrates satisfies an average growing child's nutritional needs as well as it does the adult population. This is because it meets the basic macronutrient demands for an average individual in line with the government and various health agency guidelines. Clearly, if a child is in a prolonged, extensive, physical training programme for a specific sport the help of a qualified paediatric specialist is called for. If you are concerned that your child's energy demands are not met, make sure to include nutrient-dense carbohydrate options such as potato, sweet potato, corn, and rice with meals. As for many adults, the major health concern is that children are not eating sufficient amounts of protein to meet their ongoing cellular developmental demands. A diet rich in certain carbohydrates (fries, bread, sweetened breakfast cereal, and pastries) not only fails to meet your growing child's nutritional needs but also prevents your offspring from developing a taste for healthy food. A lifelong exclusion of nutritious food, nutrient-dense protein and a variety of vegetables, is not supportive of good health outcomes.

What I soon learn is that Maya loves and craves sweets. She always has space for dessert and the sweeter the ingredients, the better. So when we look at her plate composition, we are looking at her main meal composition, which is very good. However, when we add her preference for sweets, biscuits, homemade ice cream, and desserts, we uncover a possible contributory factor when looking at why her young skin continues to be affected in such a way. Another crucial piece of information is the investigation of food allergies that her consultant paediatrician ordered back in 2012. That allergy test revealed that little Maya had an immunoglobulin E (IgE) antibody, type I hypersensitivity reaction to eggs, peanuts, and soya. Maya's mom has been monitoring Maya's reaction to different foods and has discovered that farmed salmon and all sesame seed and related products, including Tahini, result in Maya experiencing a swelling of her lips and itching in her throat. These symptoms sometimes necessitate oral steroidal treatment.

Remember that skin conditions are irrefutably linked to gut microbes and in Maya's case, a non-invasive comprehensive stool analysis showed some interesting findings. Maya's good gut bacteria profile was excellent which is reflective of her type of birth, 10-month exposure to breast milk, and varied diet. Unfortunately, she also tested positive for two different parasites and a significant amount of excess yeast. Sugar is the preferred food of these non-beneficial gut microbes and Maya's craving for sweets might very well be a contributing factor in her ongoing eczema.

## What Is the Health Issue with Sugar?

"Sugar and spice and all things nice, that's what little girls are made of." Sugar is viewed as an edible that should not form part of a daily diet when we aim to improve our health. But when we shift our focus to children it seems that doting family members, close friends, and even strangers met on the street will look for any opportunity to treat the little ones. And that excludes the many holidays such as Easter, Christmas, New Year, and birthdays where sweets, treats, and sugar fuel our younger generation at the expense of a balanced meal. Let us also remember the treats that are given to children when they visit the doctor, playgroup, and hairdresser.

Ordinary sugar is an extraordinary food substance. It is needed to activate yeast when baking bread and can transform plain flour and eggs to the most sublime of treats. From the moment we are born, our sweet tooth is developed by life-giving colostrum (first breast milk) from which we continue to be breastfed or move on to infant formula both of which contain significant and rather comparable amounts of carbohydrates. Breast-and-bottle-fed infants obtain 40% of their energy from milk sugars in the form of lactose, essential ingredients when embarking on a growth spurt.

Sugar, like all other carbohydrates, contains three atoms, carbon, hydrogen and oxygen. The term 'sugar' generally refers to monosaccharides or simple sugars (glucose, fructose and galactose) and disaccharides (sucrose, maltose and lactose). The most obvious source is sugar cane or sugar beet and is used in sweets, cakes, biscuits, desserts, soft drinks, jams and preserves, and less obviously in bread, breakfast cereals, some cold meats, and tinned goods. Historically, sugar was a commodity only obtainable by the very affluent and was consumed as the climax at the end of a dining feast. Until the 1100s, sugar was an unknown substance in Europe where it was encountered during the crusades to the holy land. It remained a luxury item until the 1700s and during the 18th century became more widely available. Its use in confectionery was now well established and England started to develop a habit for sugary sweetness. Sugar's increased production and popularity was entwined with the dark trade of slavery. Colonial rule in the West Indies saw the enslavement of millions of Africans to ensure supply met with the ever-increasing demand for this luxurious white crystal. The price we pay to meet our insatiable demand for sugar is not only linked with weight and health concerns but unfortunately includes questionable ethics as well. Global sugar production increased sevenfold between 1900 and 1964. There is no other major crop in history that can match this rate of increase.

Sugar still regularly makes the headlines albeit for very different reasons. Recently the war on sugar has been waged and informed shoppers are frantically reading nutritional information labels. Remember that glucose is the preferred fuel or energy source for cells and sugar is highly nourishing. The purer the sugar, the purer the energy. All our bodily functions require energy to perform their much-needed daily tasks. The brain, nervous system and red blood cells need glucose as a source of energy. Even whilst sleeping your body requires energy to function. Just think of your heartbeat that may slow down but your heart does not completely stop working just because you are lying in the foetal position for approximately eight hours a night. The biggest concern with sugar consumption is that we tend to eat more in calorific value than we need. Excess energy does not magically dissipate, it is stored in adipose tissue until there is a period of famine and the body can draw on those stored reserves. This is a basic survival technique, an evolutionarily adaptive trait that has served us well in the millennia where the natural state was constant near starvation.

Sugar can have effects on weight and obesity, insulin resistance and diabetes, dental caries, and micronutrient dilution. Whilst there is no clear link between the quantity of sugar consumed and dental caries, research suggests that there is a strong relationship between dental caries and the frequency of sugar consumption. In societies where the average total sugar supplies are less than 20kg/person/annum, dental caries is rare. How many times have you visited your dentist where you were asked how often you snack on traditional sweet treats? The advice is often given to only eat confectionery postprandially, i.e. after a meal. This allows for saliva to clean the teeth from excess sugar, which can feed certain unwanted, harming bacteria in the oral cavity.

When sugar-rich foods replace nutrient-dense alternatives they can displace other crucial macro and micronutrients and thus be a source of 'empty' calories. An Irish study concluded that high consumption of added sugars was associated with a decrease in the micronutrient density of the diet and increasing prevalence of dietary inadequacies in children and teenagers. Looking at Maya's diet, we can see that her meals are very well structured, but as soon as she reaches for that all-important dessert or packet of sweets, she is changing the number of nutrients that she has just gained from her food. Simplistically put, sugar robs your body of nutrients so your long-term health outcome is not only dependent on what you avoid in your diet but equally based on that which you actually eat or drink. If on a warm summer's afternoon you enjoy a vibrant, nutrient-dense salad, followed by a meringue with strawberries and cream, and then consume half a bottle of wine at the same meal, your overall nutrient status remains sub-optimal. Your chances of putting on extra weight are still significant. Your risk of developing type II diabetes remains strong. Your health status is only likely to improve if you enjoy the salad and avoid the meringue, double cream, and alcohol. The latter three ingredients are all forms of concentrated, non-essential sugar. The types of choices that are driven by emotional drives rather than actual nutritional needs.

Sugar has also been implicated in attention-deficit hyperactivity disorder (ADHD) and the Feingold diet advocates the removal of all forms of sugar and additives from affected children's diets. A comparison of relevant scientific data (meta-analysis) of 23 studies involving 560 subjects concluded that there is no direct impact of sugar on behaviour. Science aside, many teachers and parents do anecdotally report improved behaviour when sugary treats are kept to a minimum for these individuals at risk. The 'Mind For Better Mental Health' campaign advocates the minimal inclusion of sugar in the daily diet to help address symptoms of mental health, which includes depression. Depressed individuals have been shown to prefer sweet foods. Whether there is a direct link between sugar consumption and the development of depression remains without conclusive evidence. But if you look at your own experience, how many times have you felt wonderful whilst enjoying a sugar-laden snack or dessert and not long after the meal felt significantly less exuberant? Just because a government-funded scientific study has not yet been undertaken to prove or disprove the link between mood and sugar intake, does not mean sugar has been elevated to essential nutrient status.

Current UK government guideline recommendation for sugar intake is set at a maximum of 11% of the total daily food energy. That equals 60 g of sugar. In terms of teaspoon measures, 1 teaspoon = 4 g of sugar, which sets your upper limit at 15 teaspoons of sugar.

**Table 14**: Sugar content of some common foods

| Food choice | Grams of sugar | Teaspoons of sugar |
|---|---|---|
| A 30g serving of Kellogs® Cornflakes with 125ml of semi-skimmed milk | 9 | just over 2 |
| A hot beverage with 2 teaspoons of sugar | 8 | 2 |
| 2 digestive chocolate biscuits | 6 | almost 2 |
| 1 can of Heinz® Cream of Tomato soup | 19.6 | almost 5 |
| 1 part of a Mars® Duo Chocolate bar | 25.4 | almost 6 |

If these options form part of your daily intake, then you have already consumed 68 g of sugar, which equates to an excess of 8 g (2 teaspoons).

The key to eating is to be aware of the content of your food and how it will make your body work optimally, not throw a spanner in the works. If you have a sweet tooth then you owe it to your long-term health outlook to take a hard look at where you are consuming sugar in your daily diet. Sugar is not an essential nutrient and nobody needs it is their diet. To subscribe to the belief that you *need* a sugar or sweet treat only serves to make you feel better about your personal choices.

It is not unusual for us to lead a more sedentary life due to the increasing demands on our time. As the seasons change, we may be less inclined to go for a run or walk in the park and even be too time poor to visit a gym to burn off those excess grams of sugar, which can accumulate over time and lead to undesirable diseases so often reported in the news. The lack of structured exercise in schools means that even children, like Maya, may not be enjoying adequate physical movement to counter the intake of excess, empty calories in the form of sugary snacks. The fact is that sugar does not offer any health benefits. When you have a moment to reflect, ask yourself whether that extra 'spoonful of sugar really is needed to make the medicine go down'.

## Choosing Food to Address Eczema

Maya is only 9 years old and desperately wants to eat school dinners like her classmates. Given that eczema has a strong link with certain food choices and that Maya is scratching her itching skin resulting in painful sores, it is necessary to explain the link between what she chooses to eat and her skin behaviour.

**Table 15**. Foods to choose when dealing with eczema

| Food group | Option |
|---|---|
| Milk | Coconut milk only |
| Nuts | Walnuts only |
| Seeds | Hemp, flax (linseeds), pumpkin, sunflower |
| Starches | Only gluten free options such as amaranth, buckwheat, millet, quinoa, parsnip, potatoes, rice, sorghum, sweet corn, sweet potato, turnip |
| Protein | Legumes, fish, and animal flesh (no egg) |
| Vegetables | All vegetables, depending on individually confirmed allergies or sensitivities |

Maya is a bright girl and of her own accord decides that the benefit of healthy skin by far outweighs the sharing of problem foods with her peers. The key when negotiating with a patient, no matter their age, is to offer alternative options rather than focusing on what should be avoided. The fact that Maya's mother is an excellent, competent, and willing cook, means that Maya welcomes the change in diet, despite it including no dairy or gluten-containing grains at all. For Maya, the most suitable dairy alternative is coconut, in all shapes and forms from the clear liquid to desiccated coconut. Coconut cream added to soups or breakfast porridge oats not only enhances the taste it also means that Maya's system is not exposed to one of the most common gut irritants in modern times, bovine dairy. Sardines are packed with bone-building calcium and many products these days are fortified with this mineral, negating the need to focus on dairy product to meet calcium demands.

Gluten alternatives include quinoa, amaranth, buckwheat, rice, sorghum, millet, corn and gluten-free oats. We are so spoilt with the availability of excellent alternatives that we can no longer profess to being forced to eat wheat as the only available source of energy.

## Making Dietary Changes

The most fantastic aspect is that this new endeavour becomes a family affair. The whole family, including both parents and younger siblings, adopt the same changes. For any health strategy to have a lasting positive impact it is imperative that you do not dangle the proverbial forbidden fruit in view of the patient. You can only successfully avoid a problem food if you are not exposed to it. Simply hiding desserts in a cupboard because the rest of the family *need* a sugar fix is setting you up for one enormous failure, sooner or later. Similarly, going shopping on an empty stomach and ambling around the store will see you slip undesirable food options in the basket without even being conscious of your behaviour. *Always* shop with a list and leave the store as soon as you have collected everything that you have planned for. Willpower is not enough when you are changing long-standing bad eating habits. Elite athletes train according to a strict, pre-planned schedule, they do not simply amble over to the gym and hope to migrate to the right equipment.

## What Happened to Maya?

Changing Maya's diet to include more protein and vegetables was the first step. Explaining to her that sweets were negatively impacting on her gut health and how that would affect her long-term health outcome was as important as the dietary changes which she agreed to. But what about the itching, red rash, and skin lesions? There are countless expensive skin creams on the market specifically aimed at these very symptoms and yet a simple Epsom salt bath and coconut oil applied once dry seemed to heal Maya's skin perfectly. Like food choices, if we can accept that real food has been instrumental in populating the Earth and that natural remedies have been around longer than patent law, then perhaps we can start our quest for optimum health.

So how has improved nutrition impacted on Maya's life? Her incredibly supportive mother reports that Maya has emerged from her painful red cocoon to an exuberant young girl with almost unblemished skin who advocates healthy eating to anybody within hearing distance.

This is what she said:

"Mentally, Maya is much more focused on her activities. Before changing her diet, she could not sit still and concentrate on what she was doing. She would do a few things at the same time and could not finish any one of them. Today she is more focused and patient, calmer.

Maya is learning better as well. Before, when she came home from school, she would be tired. Now she has much more energy, she is more enthusiastic, and she wants to do new things. For example, she is planning bicycle trips for her brother and sister.

Maya is choosing her food as she is aware of what is good for her. She is asking questions about food and she is starting to understand why it is so important in her life.

Physically, Maya does not get any infections anymore. No more coughs and runny noses. She stays healthy and has brighter eyes."

## Take-Home Message

> ➢ Sugar is not an essential nutrient.
> ➢ Eczema is related to gut health. A comprehensive stool analysis will uncover the root cause.
> ➢ Steroidal creams and medication only suppress symptoms. Nutritious food choices offer a lasting solution.
> ➢ Food affects mood, choose wisely.
> ➢ Giving your children the opportunity to enjoy a nutritious diet from a young age will help them embrace and continue good eating habits as adults.

## Meal Ideas to Address Eczema

**Breakfast**

Gluten-free toast with sardines and a side serving of cucumber and avocado

**Lunch**

Quinoa with butternut squash, peas, carrot, and chickpeas

**Dinner**

125 g Skinless chicken with rice, broccoli, asparagus, and beetroot

**Condiments**

Add a tablespoon of good quality olive oil to raw and cooked vegetables. Other options can include flaxseed, walnut, avocado, and hempseed oils.

Refer to chapter 9 for a complete food list.

# Prepare Your Plate to Address Yeast Infections

## Peter's Story

The year is 2011 and another concerned mother contacts me with regards to the gut health of her teenage son, Peter.

*****

Peter is 15 years old with short light brown hair and ice blue eyes hidden behind black-rimmed glasses. He is smartly dressed in his school uniform and I notice from his signature tie that he attends a local academic school for boys. This school is deemed one of the top academic independent schools in the UK and I have heard how strict the teaching is to maintain a certain level of scholastic performance. This type of environment can be very stressful for an adolescent with certain aspirations. Peter speaks softly and eloquently but seems a little reserved in the presence of his mother. This is not surprising as the discussion quickly turns to his gut and bowel health, a topic which is difficult to talk about for almost anyone. Peter reluctantly explains that his bowel movements too often resemble diarrhoea and that he sometimes sees blood in his stool. He gets abdominal cramps which he thinks is worse when he has milk with his breakfast cereal and in his coffee. His mother reports that Peter has been losing weight recently despite his healthy appetite.

Peter had a textbook start to life. He was born via an unassisted, natural birth weighing a healthy 3.2 kg (7 pounds) and was exclusively breastfed for 5 months. His mother decided to introduce cow milk alternatives such as goat and soy infant formula post breastfeeding and his first solid foods were vegetables and fruit. Peter and his family followed a vegan diet for five years starting when he was three. He has had all his standard immunisations without incident or adverse reactions. With regards to childhood illnesses, he had chicken pox when he was a mere-month-old and suffered from recurring croup aged one for which he received oral steroid medication. He has been diagnosed as asthmatic and sometimes needs to use his asthma inhaler. Now, as a teenager, his food choices are a little different to his peers. He enjoys an all-inclusive diet, rich in variety with ample vegetables and some fruit. He does however really like carbohydrates in the form of rice, bread, breakfast cereal, and potatoes.

Let us have a look at Peter's plate composition to see what his diet is like.

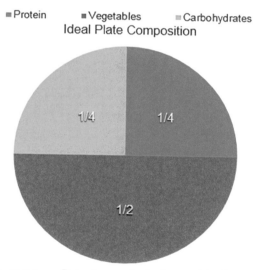

Let us compare Peter's meal choices with the ideal plate composition.

## Ideal Plate Composition

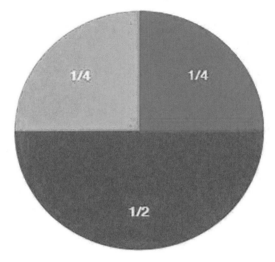

Peter is eating really well with just a little too many carbohydrate-rich options when compared to vegetables. When we consider that Peter is a growing teenager, the question that arises is, is the number of carbohydrates that he is consuming at the root cause of his current gut symptoms?

It seems that Peter's mother not only made certain personal health choices with regards to ensuring the best start in life for her son, she also continues to prepare optimal meals for her growing child. Where dependant children are concerned, food preferences are often linked with that of the parent(s) or carer. The adults' likes and dislikes are often imprinted on the children in their care and food preparation capabilities can also play a huge part. Another patient of mine, born to a mother suffering from a psychiatric condition, was raised by family members who had no interest or skill in preparing food. Up until the point where she came to see me, aged 22, vegetables and fruit were not included in her daily menu. She suffered from excruciating abdominal symptoms her whole life and has spent years under medical care to alleviate these debilitating pains. Upon inclusion of a variety of plant material, this patient reported back that her symptoms had 'miraculously' disappeared. A finding that is commonly seen in my clinical practice. Peter's problems, given his excellent diet, would not be as simple to address.

## Modern-Day Children's Diets

Children, and especially teenagers, often choose and even demand foods that include chips, pizza, and junk options such as take-out hamburgers and hotdogs. I have yet to encounter a significant number of people of any age that would choose a hearty salad over a portion of fries, and that, unfortunately, includes many health care professionals as well. How many children have you met who absolutely adore tomato sauce (ketchup)? Ask a child what their favourite meal is and chances are their response will include pizza, hamburger, sweets, chocolate milk, and ice cream. None of these choices is included in breast or infant formula milk, which all infants are exposed to for some time in their early existence. Such food choices are enforced because we present them to children on a regular basis. Given our busy lives (and mass marketing) it is deemed acceptable to insist that the family have a boxed, processed, sugared, breakfast cereal as the first meal of the day (and sometimes choose this option for the remaining two meals as well) rather than make the time, and perhaps a little more effort, to prepare an optimally nutritious meal.

These junk food meal options help people develop and nurture a very narrow taste for food, focused on carbohydrates or more specifically, sugar. Without exposure to a wider variety of foods, it is very difficult for anyone to become more adventurous when presented with unfamiliar options. Think of oysters or olives. How many people try them, and immediately enjoy the taste when they do? More often than not it takes multiple tries, and a lot of cajoling, to develop a liking for a new food, especially those options that are not overwhelmingly sweet in taste. Sweet foods are easily enjoyed by a vast majority of people. We attribute this taste preference to the composition of colostrum (first breast milk) and subsequent breast or infant formula milk. In nature, sweet tasting food (especially fruit) is rarely poisonous and because of its high carbohydrate content is an easily absorbable source of energy.

Look around you, your family, friends and work colleagues and notice how little effort it takes to prompt someone to have a biscuit, a slice of cake or any one of the little Nestle Quality Street® chocolates. But try this with a vegetable or protein option and most people will noticeably be less willing. It is our genetic programming for survival that makes it so easy for humans to choose certain options over others. But it is equally due to our questionable habits that we choose to avoid nutrient-dense food options and only source and arguably enjoy less healthy choices.

## Gut Concerns in a Growing Teenager

The main concern with Peter was his recent, drastic weight loss. When considering this in light of his loose bowel movements, which may be related to certain food choices, and the academic pressure he tells me he is under at school, the concern here is that he might be at risk of developing an inflammatory bowel disease (IBD). An ever-increasing amount of young adults are being diagnosed with Crohn's disease or ulcerative colitis, illnesses that are not only incurable but can have a significant health impact on the patient. Peter is only 15 and his future still holds a couple of notable school exams (GCSE and A-level) prior to heading off to university. All these factors supported an investigation into Peter's gut health via a comprehensive stool analysis to uncover the root cause of his presenting symptoms. With the suspicion that some foods may be exacerbating his condition, Peter decided that a blood sample test for food intolerances would be ideal.

To say that Peter's gut was in a little bit of a mess would be an understatement. Given that one of the standard gut inflammation markers was elevated and that his stool tested positive for blood, Peter was immediately referred to a consultant gastroenterologist. Fortunately the diagnosis after further testing and investigation at an esteemed hospital was IBS and not that of an inflammatory bowel disease. It transpires that Peter had very few beneficial gut flora species which would be exacerbated by stress, a physiological condition he is quite familiar with. The best means of raising levels beneficial flora is by increasing the intake of fresh vegetables in the diet. Even though Peter already enjoyed a big variety he needed to consider adding more vegetables to his plate to reflect the ideal plate composition. Peter is unlikely to be able to change his lifestyle without significantly changing his whole life plan. Peter is focused on academic achievement. He still has a few years left at school and after that, it will be a few years at university, so the stress aspect of his life is unlikely to be reduced. The best support during the coming years of study is to ensure that his gut benefits from optimum nutrition to allow his gut flora to grow and diversify in line with good health outcomes, and the primary ingredient for this is vegetables.

A further significant finding was that he had somehow contracted dysbiotic (foreign) yeast which is most notably seen in patients with either cancer or immune conditions. Extensive testing shows that only a handful of people have foreign yeast in their digestive tract and that it is coupled with an array of presenting symptoms. To dismiss yeast as a significant finding denies a patient a real solution to their undesirable symptoms. These dysbiotic yeast species thrive in an environment rich in carbohydrates and it was explained to Peter, and his mother, why this would necessitate a reduction in the amount of carbohydrate-rich foods that he eats.

When we evaluated his blood test for food sensitivities we were all surprised at the sheer number of foods that he tested positive for. The most notable finding was that dairy, as Peter himself observed, was a major component. What he did not expect was that all the obvious substitutes also tested positive. That included goat, sheep, soy, almond, and hazelnut milk alternatives. The other problematic group of foods included gluten grains, wheat and barley. Gluten is a common irritant in the gut and given the test results, he agreed to be tested for coeliac disease as well. As with the markers for IBD, this test was also negative, much to the relief of all concerned. However, given his continued diarrhoea and abdominal cramps, Peter agreed that a gluten-free diet would be a valuable inclusion especially given that there are so many naturally gluten-free starch options available to replace wheat and barley. The fact that rice, just one of the many gluten-free grains so readily available in all supermarkets and food outlets, was his favourite carbohydrate choice was not lost on Peter.

## Gluten, the Whole Story

Gluten has been named the villain in modern-day cooking by many health-conscious individuals, fitness fanatics, and internet experts. Companies who specialise in gluten-free food products are enjoying a profitable practice because now it is not only patients who have been diagnosed with coeliac disease who rely on these products. A significant number of health conscious people now choose to shop in that special 'free from' aisle.

To understand why gluten has been branded one of the most problematic foods in the standard Western diet we need to look at the mechanism which turns food into absorbable nutrients. The digestive tract runs from mouth to anus and is one long tube where the magic of digestion happens. For coeliac sufferers and gluten sensitive individuals, the major area of concern is the small intestine, the part of the digestive tract which starts just after the stomach and continues all the way to the big bowel or commonly called the colon. The small intestine is lined with finger-like protrusions, called villi, that extend its surface area and ensure that it captures all the nutrients we get from the food we eat. Gliadin, a protein part of gluten found in certain cereal grains, damages the villi in the lining of the digestive tract such that coeliac patients experience abdominal distress and discomfort. This irreparable damage to the villi leads to malabsorption of important nutrients resulting in deficiency and weight loss. These symptoms, which include diarrhoea, abdominal distress, and weight loss are all consistent with Peter's complaints.

To fully appreciate the role of the villi covering the intestine think of the distance one has to cover to complete a garden maze as opposed to walking in a straight line from the entrance at one end to the exit at the other end. The outer surface area (your abdomen) is significantly smaller in size compared to the small intestine when lifted out of the body, laid down on a flat surface and stretched out lengthwise. According to the new world encyclopaedia, the human intestine can be as long as 7 metres (23 feet). The villi in the small bowel, on average, enlarge the surface area 6.5 times and the microvilli (yes, there are micro finger-like protrusions embedded in the villi) furthermore contribute to an enlargement of 13 times the original length. The importance of increasing the surface area of the small bowel is to allow the optimal uptake of key nutrients. Think of a production line where quality assurance takes place. The more people or checkpoints on the line, the more assurances you have that the end product has been thoroughly inspected. These nutrients initiate, support, and sustain all biological functions in your complex bodily systems. Functions that allow you to blink an eye, avoid being struck in the head by a flying object, and even create a new life in the form of a baby. Nutrients that are vital in supporting Peter's growth.

Fatty diarrhoea, in which unabsorbed nutrients are excreted, is a notable symptom of coeliac disease. Nutrient deficiencies affect the body's ability to repair and grow. For children who test positive for coeliac disease that means that they do not grow as well as their healthy peers. There is no cure for coeliac disease, only dietary vigilance and avoidance of the obvious edible culprits. For gluten sensitive people, like Peter, it is best to minimise exposure to gliadin. Unlike coeliac sufferers, he does not have to completely avoid these grains because an intolerance is not an incurable disease. An intolerance signifies that a patient needs to repair any digestive damage and optimise biological function before re-introducing offending foods. For most patients, this phase of food avoidance generally lasts about three months with the correct healing protocol put in place. Peter did, however, indicate that he understood that every time he eats gluten grains and dairy and milk alternatives he increases his chances of bloody diarrhoea and abdominal cramps. He chose to address the symptoms via diet rather than ignore the warning signs and risk greater damage later on in life.

It is human nature to selectively choose what we will eat and what we will refuse. If you choose to avoid gluten for health reasons your food choices should focus on those foods that are contributory to a healthier outcome. A gluten-free cookie does not suddenly become a healthy option just because you baked it without using wheat flour. A cookie, by definition, is a non-essential food option, which contains a sweetening agent, be it sugar, artificial sweeteners, xylitol, agave syrup, stevia, molasses, fructose, or honey, and a carbohydrate-rich option in the form of rice, corn, soy, or potato flour. Even if you have added a protein option such as pecan nuts, the whole product is overwhelmingly carbohydrate-rich and can never, in all good conscience, be considered an essential nutrient-dense food. If your grandmother, who probably grew up in an era where food was viewed in a different way, did not consider it a sensible meal replacement, then neither should you, despite what the advertisements or passionate food bloggers would like you to believe.

By now, you are fully aware of the undeniable health benefits of vegetables and fruit and how crucial it is in terms of bowel health to regularly include a great variety in the diet. Both these products, in their natural form, are uniformly gluten free. If, like Peter, you choose a gluten-free diet for reasons other than confirmed coeliac disease diagnosis, the best options are to include starchy vegetables as gluten grain alternatives. Those include potatoes, turnips, corn, sweet potatoes, yams, and swedes. Amaranth, buckwheat, millet, gluten-free oats, quinoa, sorghum, and rice are all excellent gluten-free, cereal-like alternatives. Opting for these naturally gluten-free grains has the added advantage that they contain plant fibre, the role of which is essential for good gut health, the very reason Peter came to see me. The archaic view that some patients should follow a no fibre diet is no longer held by experts in the field because of the essential role fibre plays in maintaining the health of your gut bacteria and preventing bowel cancers.

## What Happened to Peter?

To support Peter, a growing young man, in terms of energy-rich, carbohydrate food options his choices are to include fruit, vegetables, and naturally gluten-free carbohydrate-rich choices. The added benefit of opting for these choices is that the financial gain is directed at farming, not food manufacturing industries, who may be more focused on annual profits than Peter's long-term health outcome. The various health foundations, including the WHO, do not significantly benefit financially from advocating diets rich in fruit and vegetables. I am always suspicious when a company has the resources to buy prime time advertisement slots in which they sing a product's praises. Impressive packaging is both an expense and an environmental burden and someone has to foot the bill. Your local farmer's market or greengrocer does not appear to have the resources to invest in such marketing ploys. An apple is an apple and you can pick one, put it in your own carrier bag and enjoy without any further preparation.

Peter not only understood the need to optimise his nutritional intake to address his dysbiotic yeast and food sensitivities he also managed to put the simple rules in practice. Our work together spanned almost one year and he not only gained an impressive 9 A* grades at GSCE, he later gained entry to his preferred university.

Half a decade after our initial contact, Peter reported the following:

"I'm glad to report that after five years my gut seems to be acting rather well. My stress in school life has been replaced with an equally healthy amount of stress at university, although I'm learning how to deal with it better. Also, with my lack of dairy options and general incompatibility with meat, I've found a good helping of inspiration in the vegan community to learn how to cook and eat all sorts of odd varieties of cereals and legumes that seem to be treating me and my bowels a lot better than bog-standard wheat. In fact, after all this time avoiding sweet treats, I never feel like eating cake, even if they're handing it out for free. I can't imagine I ever would have been able to develop my diet to a level I'm happy at without your help. Thank you."

## Take-Home Message

➢ Naturally gluten-free foods grow in abundance in nature and include:
  • Amaranth,
  • Buckwheat,
  • Corn (Maize),
  • Millet,
  • Polenta,
  • Potato,
  • Quinoa,

- Rice,
- Sorghum.

➢ Gluten-free bread, cakes, biscuits, pastries, and beer are not essential in the diet.

➢ Adolescence is a very important phase in life; if you experience any suspicious symptoms, get tested.

➢ Unexplained weight loss in young adults requires immediate investigation.

## Meal Ideas for the Young Vegan

### Breakfast
Porridge oats (made with water only) with 2 tablespoons of mixed seeds such as hempseed and flax (linseed)

### Lunch
Vegetable soup with mixed beans or lentils or chickpeas

### Dinner
Rice, stir-fry containing 125 g cubed tofu, shiitake mushrooms, broccoli, asparagus, and grated beetroot

### Condiments
Add a tablespoon of good quality olive oil to raw and cooked vegetables. Other options can include flaxseed, walnut, avocado, and hemp seed oils.

Refer to chapter 9 for a complete food list.

# Prepare Your Plate for Improved Cholesterol and Healthy Weight

## Silvia's Story

Silvia contacted me because those around her constantly remark on her weight and her physician is concerned with her elevated cholesterol.

*****

Silvia is a 30-year-old professional businesswoman who works in computing. She has slightly curly brown hair and hazel eyes hidden behind her fashionable glasses. Her skin is without any blemishes and given her Italian heritage she can easily tan to an enviable brown colour. Physically Silvia is very slight and has a fairly active lifestyle. Her body mass index (BMI) has seldom gone above 19, which is just short of the acceptable normal range of 20 to 25. BMI is still considered a good measure of health and is calculated by dividing your body weight, measured in kilograms, by the square of your height, measured in metres (BMI = weight in kg/height in metres$^2$). Silvia maintains her slender frame by dabbling in squash, tennis, beach volleyball, and on her free weekends, she often heads off to the mountains on long walking expeditions.

Her main concern, high cholesterol, is due to her family history of cardiovascular disease (CVD). High cholesterol is still medically considered a marker for CVD and anyone who undergoes a blood test and is given a result of high cholesterol will be made aware of the possible risks. We now know that cholesterol is just part of the story and results should be read alongside total triglycerides, low-density lipoprotein (LDL, termed bad cholesterol) and high-density lipoprotein (HDL, termed good cholesterol). LDL cholesterol is said to have a damaging effect on your arteries and concerns are raised with high total triglycerides and LDL levels that are significantly higher than HDL levels. A patient with high cholesterol and high HDL versus LDL is not considered at risk. Silvia's total triglyceride levels were set within the acceptable reference range, but her LDL was notably elevated when compared to her HDL levels.

We know that diet, lifestyle and obesity are all important factors to consider when minimising the risk of CVD. Silvia's weight was not a direct risk factor given that she was considered underweight for her height and age. She does not smoke nor overindulge in alcohol and her active lifestyle is reassuring. The remaining factors are diet and stress and Silvia indicated that stress was indeed a part of her life. She works long hours and travels across the globe regularly. Her home life is not without stress due to her many responsibilities surrounding her extended family as is often the case with traditional Italian families. Being raised in a close-knit family means that your time is not always your own. Let us have a look at what Silvia was eating when we first met

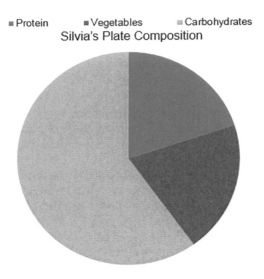

■ Protein  ■ Vegetables  ▨ Carbohydrates
Silvia's Plate Composition

Have a look again at the ideal Plate Composition for comparison.

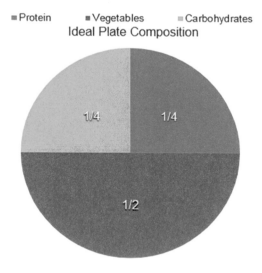

Protein  Vegetables  Carbohydrates
Ideal Plate Composition

## The Health Implications of Being Underweight

Silvia's diet was overwhelmingly focused on carbohydrates because her doctor and family members were concerned with her weight. There is still a common belief that a person who is underweight needs to increase their carbohydrate or starch intake to boost their weight. Silvia's concerned mother insisted that she eat a lot of white bread, wheat crackers, and pasta to support weight increase. In times of food scarcity, we gravitate towards anything edible to stave off starvation. Given that root vegetables and starches can grow in abundance and withstand extreme temperatures, it is often the only form of sustenance found during times of food scarcity such as war and civil unrest. To rely on an almost exclusive refined carbohydrate-rich diet to address weight concerns when other nutrient-dense food options are plentiful goes contrary to sound nutrition advice. In a way, this is a kind of reverse fad diet to losing weight.

When addressing excess weight the first step is to eliminate empty calories from the diet and, as we have seen, this can be to the detriment of indispensable nutrients. Unfortunately, too many health care professionals still insist that an underweight patient put on weight, at any cost, via a strategy that is also void of essential nutrients. Many underweight people are given a high sugar, low protein, low fibre, meal-replacement formula that is supposed to help them gain weight in the shortest time possible. The concern for Silvia with this type of ill-considered strategy is that she already has high cholesterol, which is strongly related to high intake of carbohydrates in the diet, and her father has type II diabetes. The genetic component for CVD risk in Silvia's family was very high given that her father is a diabetic, has heart disease, and lung cancer due to his many years of smoking tobacco, all serious health factors.

Silvia does not have much of an appetite when she first wakes in the morning and tends to fuel herself with a double serving of black coffee. Silvia is an avid coffee drinker with a preference for a strong espresso. Her morning routine is partly due to the fact that she only goes to sleep after midnight and wakes up tired and unrefreshed. Coffee, as expected, gives her the necessary boost to start a long working day. Hours pass before she sits down for lunch at her work canteen where she is at the mercy of the cooks' hot dish of the day. Given that the food has to be kept warm for the duration of a long lunchtime period, Silvia says that whatever vegetables might be on offer are no longer appetising by the time she is able to take her break. This means that she chooses pasta dishes with cheese more often than not. What is interesting to note is that her dinner, eaten quite late given her long commute between home and the office, contains a lot of cow dairy despite her being tested lactose intolerant by her doctor. Her preferred protein choice includes a sizeable beefsteak, cooked rare. Vegetable options do not feature regularly. Her meal choices play right into the hand of increased CVD risk.

It seems to be a misconception that all people from Mediterranean descent enjoy the kind of foods that are repeatedly shown to promote good heart health, such as fresh fish, legumes, plenty freshly picked vegetables, and the pièce de résistance, liberal helpings of extra virgin olive oil. The newly updated Italian food guidelines state that a person should eat as follows:

**Table 16.** Italian food guidelines

| To include at all meals | On a daily basis | On a weekly basis |
| --- | --- | --- |
| 1-2 portions of fruit | 2-3 portions of milk and milk products | 1-2 portions of poultry |
|  |  | >2 portions of fish and seafood |
| >2 portions of vegetables | 1-2 portions of fruit, seeds, olives | 2-4 portions of egg |
|  |  | >2 portions of legumes |
| 1-2 portions of bread, pasta, rice, or couscous | 3-4 portions of olive oil | < 2 portions of meat |
|  |  | <1 portion of cold meats |
|  | Herbs, spices, garlic, and onion | <2 portions of dessert |

The Italian food guidelines, traditional food pyramid, and NHS EatWell plate all advocate a diet which contains a large percentage of carbohydrates in the form of cereals to be consumed at every meal. Silvia's food choices of pasta and bread conform to these guidelines. Interestingly enough when we look at her intake of vegetables, fruit, legumes, and fish, it seems that the message of what constitutes a healthy Mediterranean diet has somewhat been selectively ignored. When it comes to interpreting guidelines it is easy to only put on your own plate what you actually enjoy eating. In the words of the singer Meatloaf, 'two out of three ain't bad' or in Silvia's case one out of many.

## Cholesterol and Diet

To uncover why Silvia's current plate composition was a risk factor when looking at her tested high cholesterol, let us look at the role of cholesterol in the human body. Cholesterol, made mainly in the liver, is a very important fat-like substance that we find in our cells. Cholesterol is responsible for the formation of your stress hormones, sex hormones, and bile salts, which help you break down fats in the diet. When your body does not manufacture bile salts and you are unable to break down fats in the diet, you run the risk of preventing the absorption of the fat-soluble vitamins (A, D, E, and K) from your food. Having insufficient fat-soluble vitamin uptake can cause a range of health problems (see table 13 below). Additionally, without cholesterol, you run the risk of imbalanced sex hormones, low stress hormones, and low micronutrient status.

**Table 13**. Fat-soluble micronutrients linked with function and food source

| Micronutrient | Function | Food source |
|---|---|---|
| Vitamin A | • Vision, notably night vision<br>• Growth and development<br>• Fertility<br>• Immune support<br>• Anti-oxidant | • Organ meats<br>• Dairy products<br>• Dark leafy green vegetables<br>• Yellow and orange vegetables<br>• Fortified products |
| Vitamin D | • Absorption of calcium, which plays an essential part in bone health.<br>• Low bone density can lead to osteoporosis. | • Cod liver oil<br>• Cold-water fish (mackerel, salmon, and herring)<br>• Butter<br>• Egg yolks<br>• Fortified dairy<br>• Dark green leafy vegetables |
| Vitamin E | • Anti-oxidant<br>• Immune function | • Vegetable oils<br>• Seeds<br>• Nuts<br>• Whole grains<br>• Fortified products |

| Micronutrient | Function | Food source |
| --- | --- | --- |
| Vitamin K | • Blood clotting<br>• Bone health | • Dark leafy green vegetables<br>• Green tea<br>• Oats<br>• Whole wheat |

Cholesterol only becomes a health concern when levels in your body become too elevated and certain food choices play a major role. The obvious culprits are high carbohydrate intake, sugar, caffeine, fats such as margarine and other trans-fats and hydrogenated vegetable oils, and full-fat milk products such as milk, cream, cheese, and yoghurt. Other risk factors associated with excess cholesterol include a low fibre diet and impaired liver function. Because cholesterol is made in the liver it is also very important for a person to have their liver working unhindered. Medication, of all sorts, can put an extra burden on liver function and Silvia's medical history reveals that she takes antihistamine tablets for debilitating seasonal hayfever, a steroidal inhaler for asthma, and is on the oral contraceptive pill. Even though this does not sound like a lot when it comes to liver function every foreign substance (that which comes from outside of our bodies) makes extra work for this large, essential organ.

Have another look at Silvia's plate composition and note how few vegetables she eats. Vegetables are an excellent source of fibre and essential nutrients and help lower cholesterol, so a lack thereof in Silvia's diet is a major concern. Being prescribed a cholesterol-lowering drug, such as statins, should surely only occur when all dietary avenues have been exhausted and proved ineffective. Once you start on this type of medication, you are going to be taking it for the rest of your life. Not only is this a sizeable, long-term financial expense, it is also linked with undesirable side-effects and may impair all those hormones and nutrients that rely on cholesterol. Even though there is a genetic component to high cholesterol for some diet and lifestyle choices are far more significant. Parameters that you can change and manage.

Silvia's carbohydrate choices of white pasta, bread, and wheat crackers are not known for their fibre content. In fact, these options are often recommended for patients who need to follow a low fibre diet. Crackers often contain hydrogenated vegetable oils, a big contributor to high cholesterol. Not only does Silvia have a genetic predisposition to CVD, her diet lacks fibre, she has a high coffee intake, is stressed, and takes an array of medication which all exacerbate her current high cholesterol status. On the plus side, Silvia has an active lifestyle, is not overweight, and very importantly does not smoke. As for IBD and PMS, smoking is a major risk factor for high cholesterol and ultimately CVD. If you are still smoking please make a concerted effort to kick this bad habit. Not just for the environment but ultimately to ensure that you have a better long-term health outlook.

Silvia's doctor had diagnosed her with lactose intolerance early in 2009 and shortly after she decided to embark on an elimination (oligoantigenic) diet to identify further food triggers given that her symptoms had not disappeared once she switched to lactose-free milk products.

## Stress and Weight Loss

Before Silvia's health troubles began her weight was stable at 63 kg (9 st 9) (a normal BMI of 20). The first turning point saw her weight reduced to 55 kg (8 st 7) (BMI of 17). In the two years that had passed since Silvia originally sought my help, she managed to increase her weight to 58 kg (9 st 1) (BMI of 18). In January 2011, after an unexpected personal crisis, Silvia suffered from the most debilitating stomach cramps, which left her without appetite and suffering from nausea. She was rapidly losing weight (weighing just 48 kg (7 st 6), BMI of 15) and her bowel movements had progressed to watery diarrhoea. After an emergency gastroscopy, her consultant prescribed repeated doses of antibiotics for suspected bacterial infection. She was also instructed to continue with her daily dose of Omeprazole, a commonly used antacid (proton pump inhibitor or PPI), which she had been taking since 2009. Her situation did not improve and given that she was not tested to confirm a specific bacterial infection she contacted me again and decided to complete a comprehensive stool analysis. Even though she had identified a few problematic foods via her elimination diet prior to seeing me in 2009, Silvia decided that she would prefer to complete a food intolerance screen to identify food irritants quickly.

When someone's bowel misbehaves like Silvia's, the diagnosis is often IBS and after a round or two of antibiotic treatment, traditionally no further investigation is deemed necessary. In my clinic, I have seen IBS caused by any of the following: parasitic or bacterial or yeast (Candida) infection and food sensitivities. A comprehensive stool analysis revealed that Silvia had low levels of the good bacteria, *Lactobacillus*. This comes as no real surprise as the stress in Silvia's life had not yet been alleviated and a direct correlation between prolonged stress and a reduction in this type of beneficial flora has already been established by the scientific community. Beneficial gut flora protects against infections and plays an integral part in the transit time of food through the big bowel (colon). Too few beneficial gut flora may result in constipation much like a low fibre diet. The most important finding was that Silvia tested negative for *Helicobacter pylori,* a common bacteria that can affect the delicate balance of the many bacteria residing in the gut and for which Omeprazole is commonly prescribed. Silvia has been on this antacid medication for more than two years and given that her test results for *Helicobacter pylori* were negative it was time to consider the option of discontinuing its use. With the absence of any bacterial infection, Silvia approached her consultant and they agreed that it was futile to continue with her medication. Silvia's blood food sensitivity screen revealed a few problem foods and upon in-depth discussion, she decided to eliminate the tested food culprits and to introduce a variety of safe, nutritious alternatives.

The most immediate concern here was that Silvia was losing weight rapidly and this is not ideal for her long-term health outcome. For a lot of patients increasing their weight can be as difficult as an obese person trying their best to shed the unwanted extra pounds. Your genetic make-up plays an integral part in your body composition. Some people, like Silvia, are just naturally slim compared to their peers. Exercise plays a huge part in how your body will look and given that Silvia is no couch potato, any form of high-intensity aerobic exercise will further contribute to weight loss. Personal trainers who are the experts in the field will quickly advise an underweight client to embark on weight training instead. This kind of isometric exercise is designed to help your body build muscle mass, which is the healthy way to increase your weight.

Simply focusing on refined carbohydrates like white bread, pastries, cakes, sweets, and extra sugar in your tea or coffee is not the ideal solution for underweight patients. Not only are we aware that Silvia is prone to high cholesterol (exacerbated by a high carbohydrate diet) and genetically predisposed to CVD, we are also aware that her beneficial gut bacteria profile is far from perfect. What Silvia needs more than instant calories to boost her weight is a variety of plant matter, not only to provide much-needed fibre to remove excess cholesterol from her body but also to help increase her beneficial gut bacteria. The American and British Gut microbiome projects show how vegetables enhance the diversity of human gut bacteria and Silvia is not immune to these scientific findings. But there is another nutrient that we needed to consider to help Silvia address her sub-optimal weight: fat, and to be more precise, essential fat. Have you noticed that we only refer to amino acids, vitamins, minerals, and fats as essential? Carbohydrates or starches are not termed essential. We encountered the concept of essential nutrients when you saw how important protein in the diet was for Stephen. To reiterate, when you hear the word essential pertaining to nutrition, it means that you have to eat those particular nutrients as the body is unable to derive them from other nutrients. Carbohydrates, unlike protein and certain fats, can be made from other nutrients in the body so you actually do not need them in your diet. That is a scientific fact, ask anyone who has done A-level biology.

## Fat: Enemy of the Diet Industry?

Fat elicits wide attention, both in the media and when you find yourself shopping for food. The mere mention of an avocado, a high-fat, calorie-dense option, makes people run for the hills. So acute is the aversion to fat that the thought of consuming nuts, another high-fat option, is akin to an aesthetic death sentence, a body-conscious individual's worst nightmare. Fat content is probably one of the few reasons why the majority of people glance at food labels. For those shoppers with limited time seeing the words 'low fat' or 'no fat' on the label results in an immediate purchase because it makes one believe that you have chosen the best product. For others, with more time on their hands and a desire to perhaps be better informed, there might be an in-depth study of the nutritional facts on the back of a product before deciding which one would be the superior choice. However, a quick analysis of three food products, avocado, low-fat yoghurt, and croissant, reveals intriguing results as seen below.

**Table 18.** Nutrient content of avocado compared to two other food products

| Nutritional information | Avocado per 100 g | Low fat yogurt per 100 g | Croissant per 100 g |
|---|---|---|---|
| Calories | 190 | 250 | 360 |
| Total fat | 19.5 g | 3 g | 10.3 g |
| Saturated fat | 4.1 g | 2 g | 6.5 g |
| Cholesterol | 0 | 10 mg | 75 mg |
| Sodium | 6 mg | 142 mg | 208 mg |
| Total carbohydrate | 1.9 g | 47 g | 38.3 g |
| Dietary fibre (Englyst method) | 3.4 g | 0 g | 1 g |
| Sugars | 0 | 47 g | 1.6 g |
| Protein | 1.9 g | 11 g | 8.3 g |

The biggest driving force behind fat awareness is body weight concerns. Fat intake equals a fat body, and a fat body increases your risk of cardiovascular disease. That is the message filtering down from doctors, internet 'specialists', and popular media. Did you notice the different cholesterol values of each of the foods in table 3? Were you surprised to see that an avocado does not contain any cholesterol and has the highest amount of dietary fibre? For Silvia, an avocado seems to be the perfect meal addition.

During the 1980s fitness gurus and health experts advocated the indiscriminate limitation of all fats in the diet, which set in motion the 'anti-fat revolution'. The disconcerting after-effect is that the incidence of obesity, from childhood to adults, has increased on a Global scale, particularly in societies where the Western or standard American/British diet has been adopted. This development has left qualified nutritional experts fighting a losing battle in informing the general public about the essential nature of fats. Not only is the elimination of fats in the diet correlated with an increase in weight, which puts patients at risk of developing CVD, it is also linked with a rise in learning disabilities such as dyslexia and the expanding range of attention deficit disorders. Dr Alex Richardson, from Oxford University, continues to research this area in childhood development extensively and tirelessly campaigns for the inclusion of essential fats, especially in children's diets.

Clearly, there are fats that are linked to the development of a multitude of diseases and symptoms, but we also find fats that are conducive to positive long-term health outcomes. The fats that we are warned about, by the NHS Live Well campaign and the American Heart organisation, are the saturated fats found in:

- X  fatty cuts of meats,
- X  meat products, including sausage and pies,
- X  butter, ghee, and lard,
- X  cheese, especially the hard varieties,
- X  cream,
- X  ice cream,
- X  some savoury snacks,
- X  chocolate confectionery,
- X  biscuits, cakes and pastries,
- X  palm oil,
- X  coconut oil and cream.

## The Role of Essential Fats

Essential Fatty Acids (EFAs), on the other hand, play a major role in cardiovascular health and stroke by raising high-density lipoproteins (HDL) and lowering low-density lipoproteins (LDL). HDL is commonly known as 'good' cholesterol and LDL is referred to as 'bad' cholesterol. Other benefits believed to be associated with EFAs include a decrease in bone loss (osteoporosis), a reduction in symptoms of arthritis by decreasing inflammation, promotion of wound healing, and improvement of skin conditions such as psoriasis, eczema and acne. All of these afflictions already have a host of pharmaceutical aids specifically designed to address each disorder, however, it is always worthwhile to enquire as to which foods could also help ease presenting symptoms.

There is no doubt that the inner workings of our biology are incredibly complex and that good food choices are fundamental in supporting optimal function. As advanced as the research is, all the elements of food and its interaction with our physiology is not yet completely uncovered. Food can be a powerful tool in disease prevention and recovery from illness but if we continue to view nutrition as an alternative rather than a primary therapy, we will carry on cultivating a population who depends on medication, at considerable, escalating cost.

## Gaining Healthy Weight

Silvia needed food options to help her put on healthy weight and given that we are looking for food options that will minimise her risk of CVD the following options are ideal:

- ✓ Raw and unsalted seeds and nuts, particularly hemp seeds, flaxseeds, sunflower
- ✓ seeds, pumpkin seeds, almonds, and walnuts,
- ✓ Seed and nut butters,
- ✓ Avocado,
- ✓ Flaxseed oil,
- ✓ Oily fish such as sardines, mackerel, trout, salmon, and tuna.

All of these choices contain essential fatty acids and some contain a healthy dose of protein (seeds, nuts, fish), thereby killing two birds with one stone, so to speak. You can see that when Silvia opts for these protein options to make up ¼ of her plate and adds avocado and olives, which contribute to the required ½ a plate of vegetable options, she is choosing not only the ideal plate composition but foods that help address her high cholesterol and help her increase her weight healthily. These choices support the scientific findings of a healthy

Mediterranean diet, which is irrefutably shown to minimise risks associated with CVD.

When we purely focus on weight increase, Silvia's additional options include:

- ✓ Coconut in all forms (fresh, cream, milk, desiccated),
- ✓ Eggs,
- ✓ Chicken thighs,
- ✓ Duck,
- ✓ Lamb,
- ✓ Beef.

## What Happened to Silvia?

Silvia saw an almost immediate improvement in her symptoms once she implemented the agreed dietary changes. She has not had any debilitating symptoms since March 2011 and even though she still struggles to increase her body weight (current BMI is 18), she is keeping it even and we agreed that her newfound passion for a midday swim and competitive football probably has something to do with that. Her total cholesterol has tested well within the normal range (with improved HDL and lower LDL levels) but the sad news that her father had passed away due to a blood clot in his brain following a stroke, means that Silvia continues to be very vigilant and through diet strives to minimise her risk. She understands that disease is not the inevitable outcome just because you have a genetic predisposition. In order for those genes to definitively cause you harm, your diet and lifestyle also need to be sub-optimal to help gene expression. Changing those two factors means that you can minimise your risk greatly.

Silvia gave the following feedback 6 years after our last contact:

"After adopting the dietary plan that you gave me the immediate benefits were that I was no longer nauseous after eating and as a result, I stopped vomiting. The burning feeling I normally woke up with had also disappeared. The setback I experienced in 2011 due to stress overload meant my stomach problems came back with a vengeance. I had not been following the dietary changes at the time and I believe this was my downfall. What kills me is coffee because I can feel the impact it has on my stomach. I should completely cut coffee out of my diet, but I have not managed to do that yet. When I'm careful with what I eat and drink the situation is completely under control and my weight remains stable."

## Take-Home Message

➤ Stop smoking.
➤ Being underweight is a health risk. A diet rich in refined carbohydrates and starches is not the best long-term solution.
➤ Fat is an essential nutrient. Accept it, and learn to prepare, eat, and enjoy it.
➤ You cannot change your genetic make-up. Reduce your risks of developing a disease by addressing your diet and lifestyle choices.
➤ Before you reach for long-term medication explore dietary changes to address high cholesterol.
➤ When it comes to CVD, diet is not an alternative therapy, it is *the* primary therapy;
➤ A high carbohydrate diet is not conducive to cardioprotective cholesterol output.
➤ Caffeine is an irritant in the gut. When you have a sensitive stomach switch to herbal alternatives.

## Meal Ideas to Increase Weight and Maintain Healthy Cholesterol Levels

**Breakfast**
1 Slice of rye bread with 2 scrambled eggs (add 1 tablespoon of coconut cream), olives and avocado
**Lunch**
3 New potatoes mixed with butternut squash, beetroot, and 2 chicken thighs
**Dinner**
125 g grilled trout with sweet potato, broccoli, and asparagus
**Condiments**

Add a tablespoon of good quality olive oil to raw and cooked vegetables. Other options can include flaxseed, walnut, avocado, and hempseed oils.

Refer to chapter 9 for a complete food list.

# Action Plan for
# Optimum Nutrition

## Make the Change

In this book, you have met a wonderful group of people of different ages, with diverse lifestyles that, like you, felt it was time to make a real, lasting change. Each person had a different story to tell and their motivation to look for answers and explore a simple and realistic plan either involved a specific medical diagnosis or a series of unwanted symptoms. Heather, Lawrence, and Silvia all came with a definitive diagnosis – ranging from depression, Crohn's disease, and high cholesterol – given by their respective doctors. Jenni, Stephen, and Maya all presented with unwanted skin conditions. Acne, psoriasis, and eczema are all very different afflictions and yet each patient tested positive for gut dysbiosis. Heather, Lawrence, Stephen, Peter, and Silvia needed to address their weight concerns. And we saw the impact of stress in the lives of each one of these patients.

You may find that you identify with one, more, or all of the symptoms presented by the cases in this book, and have already found help and support in the preceding chapters. You may have one or two of the symptoms, but not necessarily all of them. You may simply be aware that your diet is not as good as it could be, and know that your long-term health would benefit greatly from improved nutrition, making you the best that you can be. Whatever your nutritional needs or motivation for improved health, this chapter is about the practical steps you need to take to achieve optimal nutrition.

The people, whose stories you have read in the preceding chapters, have shown the incredible health impact this simple plate composition strategy can elicit. This group of people is not superhuman, they could be you, your mother, sibling, child, or best friend. They too handle day to day living complete with unforeseen difficulties and stress and decided to seek help and embrace the ideal plate composition. Their stories show that this straightforward, realistic plan is maintainable over the long-term and that the health benefits are motivation enough to inspire the people around you as well. Yes, there are some individuals that can wine, dine, and party without limits and still maintain excellent health. Chances are that you are not one of these statistical anomalies. You can only be your best self when your body is optimally nourished.

Food holds an emotional power over us and it can be very difficult to break that emotional chain, accept that your meal choices are sub-optimal, and implement those much-needed modifications. Unless you are in the enviable position to have a qualified chef take care of all your meals, changing your eating habits involve planning, extra work, and perseverance to reap the benefits. Just like deciding to embark on an exercise regime, the transition will take time before it stops hurting (physically and emotionally) and help you see and feel the transformational shift. It is easy to adopt a bad habit – you simply stop going for your morning run, or choose a doughnut instead of an apple at snack time – and it takes some time to embrace and cement a good habit into your daily routine. In my experience, it takes about 21 uninterrupted days for a new endeavour to become an ingrained part of your life. I believe that you can teach an old dog new tricks, the learning experience might just take a little longer. Given that dietary improvement can have such a significant long-term benefit it is most definitely worth it. Remember that you are only changing your food choices, not your eating patterns. You will still be enjoying three meals and a snack or two if you so wish.

The key to success is food. Real food, which when viewed on a plate, follows the simple rule of ½ **Vegetables**, ¼ **Protein**, and ¼ **Carbohydrates**.

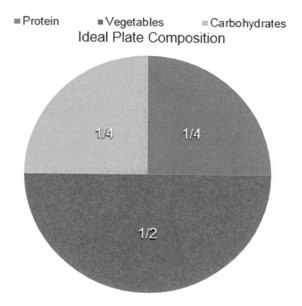

■ Protein    ■ Vegetables    ▪ Carbohydrates

**Ideal Plate Composition**

## What Changes Can You Expect?

As you embark on any healthy lifestyle change, your body needs time to adjust, physiologically and emotionally. Do not expect overnight success. Slow and steady improvements in health are more realistic and sustainable.

Your symptoms may worsen in the first week or two. This may be partly due to withdrawal symptoms from addictive or repetitive foods. It is also often due to the body using this new found supply of optimum nutrition to get rid of the toxins that may have built up after years of exposure to pollution, inadequate diet, nutrient deficiencies, and daily stress. Most people experience better health within a month.

Your commitment to these uncomplicated dietary changes makes all the difference. Eating well is a lot like learning to ride a bicycle; it takes patience, consistency, and endurance. If you falter, focus on making your next meal in line with the ideal plate composition. Dwelling on past eating indiscretions is a futile exercise. Changing dietary habits takes time and this is not a contest to see how 'good' you are. The motivation for improving your food choices is based on the realisation that good health and longevity is not a rite of passage. The more time and effort you spend on improving your health, the better the outcome.

Before introducing your new dietary strategy it is advisable to take a bit of time for menu planning and buying of the appropriate foods. Shopping on an empty stomach may lead to unhealthy impulse buys, which removes you further from your intended goal. When shopping, we are instinctively drawn to foods that invoke good memories and feelings and for most of us that include non-essential snacks, pastries, and sweets. You might be tempted to opt for a ready meal because you feel time-poor. The trick here is to familiarise yourself with meal ideas that take about as long to prepare as it does to reheat a sub-optimal pre-packaged option. Salads and stir-fried meals take only but a few minutes to prepare and will conform to the ideal plate composition. If you feel that you are too weak from hunger to wait that long, drink a large glass of water and enjoy a few olives, carrots, cherry tomatoes, avocados, mixed nuts, or even a slice of cold meat to put those hunger pangs at bay until your nutrient-dense meal is ready. Creating the ideal eating environment such as a designated dining area away from distractions – telephones and television sets – is as important as the food you eat. Eating on the run or whilst distracted is never ideal.

At the onset of changing your diet keep detailed notes of your eating and drinking habits. This can be encouraging and highlight weak areas, which may need extra care. If you are able, take photos of some of your meals as this can help you see your progress. Do you manage to follow the ideal plate composition and are your meals inclusive of a great variety and vibrant, natural colours? Many people have one or two preferred food choices that they eat over and over. Taking photos or indeed writing down what you eat will help you understand your eating behaviour. Few people are gifted with infallible memories and for most of us, it is easy to forget details surrounding our choices. Like shopping with a list, keeping a food diary and taking photos helps establish and reinforce good habits.

Let me show you how you can start your nutrition journey and implement practical changes.

## Food Shopping List

When shopping for food it is important to have a list at hand and have had something to eat. Mindless shopping and being hungry make you reach for sub-optimal and impetuous options so you end up with few nutrient-dense foods and one too many undesirable treats.

When it comes to modifying your diet it is best to avoid easy access to empty calories and minimise your need to exercise self-control. When we are hungry we are tempted to eat whatever is in sight and within easy reach. If you have non-essential treats laying around the house you might find your willpower fly out the window. The best way to entice you to eat nutritious food is to ensure that it is easily visible and in abundance. Put a stocked fruit bowl in plain sight. Keep vegetables chilled on the most visible shelf in the fridge.

The list below is your gold standard for nutrient-dense options. It clearly does not include *every* available vegetable, protein, or carbohydrate option and is compiled of the most important nutrient-dense choices. Carry it with you at all times so that it is your first point of reference when out buying food for the day or week. Cross off unsuitable choices (moral, religious, and health reasons) and focus on the remaining options. You are aiming for a diverse diet to promote positive long-term health outcomes. The science supporting gut function and health benefits in terms of varied dietary options is overwhelming and irrefutable. It is also imperative that you strive to meet the government guidelines of 5-a-day, with particular emphasis on vegetables. There is not one recent study that negates the nutritional benefits of eating vegetables, whereas there are many conflicting reports on other parts of the human diet, including red wine, coffee, fat, fish, and meat. Be adventurous and choose a variety of vibrant green, red and orange coloured vegetable options to maximise your health.

Refer to your menu plan and dietary diary. Writing down information is a powerful tool in assessing your progress, motivation, and realisation of your ultimate goals. The aim of this exercise is to draw your attention to increasing the diversity of your weekly eating preferences. When you have decided to change your past shopping habits, a list based on planned menus both ease your shopping anxiety and saves you time. I, personally, always make a shopping list on my phone (given that I never leave home without it) and follow a well-trodden path through the fresh produce section and past the meat and fish counters. Yes, I have grains in my cupboards, but those items last so long I probably only need to walk down that aisle once a month. A similar pattern exists around cold pressed oils. A large bottle of extra virgin olive oil lasts much longer than a head of Chinese leaf and I do not need to linger in the condiment section of the supermarket.

**Table 19**. Food options based on nutrient-dense and dairy free choices

| Vegetables (half a plate) | Protein (a quarter of a plate) | Carbohydrates (a quarter of a plate) |
|---|---|---|
| Artichoke | Aduki beans* | Amaranth** |
| Asparagus | Butter beans* | |
| Aubergine | Fava beans* | Barley |
| Avocado | Flageolet beans* | |
| Beetroot | Haricot beans* | Buckwheat** |
| Broccoli | Mung beans* | |
| Brussel sprouts | Red kidney beans* | Millet** |
| Cabbage | | |
| Carrot | Chickpeas* | Oats |
| Cauliflower | Lentils* | |
| Celeriac | Tofu* | Polenta** (ground corn) |
| Celery | | |
| Chard | Almonds* | Potato** (1 medium sized) |
| Chicory | Brazil nuts* | |
| Chinese Leaf | Cashew* | Quinoa** |
| Collards (brassica) | Hazelnuts* | |
| Cress | Pistachio* | Rice**: |
| Cucumbers | Walnuts* | • Basmati |
| Fennel | | • Black |
| Kale | Hempseeds* | • Brown |
| Kohlrabi (brassica) | Flaxseeds (linseeds)* | • Wild |
| Leek | Pumpkinseeds* | |
| Lettuce | Sesame seeds* | Rye |

| Vegetables (half a plate) | Protein (a quarter of a plate) | Carbohydrates (a quarter of a plate) |
| --- | --- | --- |
| Mangetout | Sunflower seeds* | Sorghum** |
| Okra | | Spelt (a type of wheat) |
| Onions | Eggs (chicken, duck, quail) | |
| Parsnip | | |
| Peas | Halibut | |
| Peppers | Herring | |
| Pumpkin | Mackerel | |
| Radicchio | Sardines | |
| Radish | Salmon | |
| Samphire (sea asparagus) | Trout | |
| Shallot | Tuna | |
| Spinach | | |
| Squash | Chicken | |
| String beans | Duck | |
| Sugar Snap Peas | Pheasant | |
| Swede | Pigeon | |
| Sweetcorn | Turkey | |
| Sweet potato | | |
| Tomato | Beef | |
| Turnip | Lamb | |
| Watercress | Pork | |
| Yam | Venison | |
| Zucchini (courgette) | | |

*Vegan protein     ** Gluten free carbohydrates

Remember all vegetables are naturally vegan and gluten-free.

## Condiments

The preceding gold standard list of nutrient-dense food options do not include condiments and dressings. Given that this book focuses on optimum nutrition, it will not promote the use of certain commercial products. Commercial sauces and condiments such as salad dressings, ketchup (tomato sauce), brown sauce, and mayonnaise often contain undesirable additions such as sugar, sweetener, salt, and low-grade quality oils. You are obviously free to enhance the flavour of your food based on your unique taste preferences.

If you strive for optimum nutrition then the best additions are good quality oils such as:

- ✓ extra virgin olive oil,
- ✓ flaxseed oil,
- ✓ avocado oil,
- ✓ walnut oil.

These oils are available in most supermarkets and not exclusively found in speciality health stores. Simply add a tablespoon serving to your salad or cooked vegetables once the meal is served. To cook, use coconut oil, ghee, butter, or other seed oils, depending on your preferences. Better yet, invest in a non-stick pan to minimise the need for greasing.

Here are a few condiment ideas to help you start on your journey.

**Simple dressing**

Mix olive oil, crushed raw garlic and chillies with a dash of lime juice. Enhance with salt, pepper or a variety of herbs depending on your audience and own taste preferences.

**Homemade mayonnaise**

2 egg yolks

1 teaspoon mustard powder 1 teaspoon salt

1 cup olive oil

A dash of cayenne pepper

A pinch of ground black pepper

Juice of 1 medium-sized lemon

Mixed herbs depending on your taste preferences

Place the egg yolks in a blender with the dry ingredients and blend well. Add the lemon juice slowly. Add the olive oil slowly while continuing to blend the mixture. You might need to add a teaspoon of boiling water to dilute the mixture if you prefer a more liquid version.

**Red pepper mayonnaise**
300 g red bell peppers
A pinch of salt
100 ml vegetable oil of your preference
Juice from a small lemon
1 teaspoon origanum
Coarsely chop the peppers and place in a small pot. Add the salt. Simmer for about 15 minutes with the lid on. Drain all the liquid. Puree the mix and gradually add the oil slowly as you would for regular mayonnaise. Lastly, add the lemon juice and origanum.

## Herbs and Spices

Herbs and spices have been used for generations as medicine and flavour enhancers. Their origin can be traced back almost to the start of civilisation. Once explorers mastered the ability to navigate ships between continents the value and use of these flavour enhancers soared and became a much sought after commodity. A whole new world of expanding medicinal cures, taste sensations, and preservative options opened up and people were prepared to pay top currency for a share. Like the introduction of sugar, these crops soon became much sought after items, revolutionising food enjoyment everywhere. These days herbs and spices are abundantly available and cultural cuisines are easily identified by the regular inclusion of certain choices. Blends of cumin, cardamom, coriander, turmeric, mustard and cayenne pepper instantly transport you to the taste of a spicy Indian curry. Mexican tacos and burritos are flavoured with garlic, onion, chilli peppers, paprika, cumin and salt. And the Italian favourite of pasta all'Arrabbiata brings forth the aromatic blend of garlic, chilli, parsley and basil leaves.

Given that flavouring is such an integral part of national identity, recipe integrity and personal preferences, it would be arrogant for anyone to suggest that food should be prepared without these important ingredients. The key to optimum nutrition is to structure your plate to include ½ Vegetables, ¼ Protein, and ¼ Carbohydrates chosen from the list of foods given above. Flavour enhancing herbs and spices are left to you to add as you wish.

We cannot, however, apply this rule to salt given that health agencies have warned about the excessive use of this common crystal. The best way to minimise your salt intake is to use only a pinch when cooking and to add other fragrant herbs and spices as primary flavour enhancers instead. Ready meals often contain added salt and it is in your best interest to make your own meals rather than depend on these time-saving options on a regular basis. It is worth re-educating your palate and learning to love the taste of vegetables without needing to enhance the flavour. A good quality extra virgin olive oil is packed with intense flavour and drizzling some on salads, cooked vegetables, jacket potatoes, and grains should realistically be enough to tantalise your taste buds.

My clinical observational data strongly suggests that people who suffer from skin afflictions – psoriasis, acne, or eczema – should avoid chilli and garlic. If you regularly experience bloating and abdominal discomfort around meals, you should ideally steer clear of onions and garlic. And if you have low blood pressure, be careful when eating raw garlic as this is a century-old remedy, effective at lowering blood pressure.

## Mushrooms

Mushrooms are lauded as a highly nutrient-dense food and some people classify them as vegetables. Botanically speaking, mushrooms are fungi and if you are to believe the plethora of popular literature they are the holy grail of edibles. Claims of anti-obesity, cancer, and diabetes properties are well publicised. Provided you do not wander into a forest and forage mushrooms without being able to distinguish between food and poison, mushrooms add a distinctive flavour to many dishes. Think of porcini used in Italian risotto, portobello mushrooms as a meat substitute in hamburgers, shiitake in Japanese Miyabi (clear onion soup), and button mushrooms in French omelettes. Remember that mushrooms are not vegetables, so do not be tempted to replace your vegetable portion on your plate. Unless you have a confirmed yeast infection, dislike the taste, or have a mushroom sensitivity, you can enhance your meals with mushrooms provided that you always adhere to the ideal plate composition.

# Fruit

Fruit is nature's gift in terms of fibre, flavour, micronutrients and ease of enjoyment. It makes for excellent snack options and breakfast additions. But, unlike vegetables, it is not a fundamental component of the human diet. When it comes to juice options, health agencies warn that you can replace only one portion of your 5-a-day with a fruit juice. The reason for this warning is that extracted fruit juices not only remove the fibre component of the fruit, it also supplies a concentrated form of sugar. Both of these components are contrary to sound nutrition advice. Eating a fresh fruit is preferred to drinking fruit juice or choosing dried fruit, but even then, it is not essential. If you do not have a sweet tooth and do not already like eating fruit, there is no reason why you should re-educate your palate to regularly include fruit in your diet. For optimum nutrition, it is still best to focus on a diverse variety of vegetables rather than make main meals which consist exclusively of fruit. Many people find that fruit can exacerbate bloating and other digestive symptoms especially when eaten after a meal. I always advocate eating these wonderful options on an empty stomach or between meals, in moderation.

# Dessert

Doting grandparents and ad campaigns alike feel the need to entice us to indulge in treats at every possible occasion. From an individually wrapped boiled sweet to a rich triple chocolate, multiple-tiered cake, the focus on treats and sweet foods, deemed imperative for special occasions, has created an industry that is difficult to avoid. Whereas family members associate treats with expressing love, the growing cake and sweet industry is driven by profit. No health agency endorses the daily consumption of sweets and treats. Our insatiable hunger for desserts is allowing these commercial enterprises to permeate every facet of modern-day living. Phrases like 'A Mars™ a day helps you work, rest and play', 'Have a break, have a Kit Kat™', and 'If cupcakes are wrong. We don't wanna be right' are omnipresent via billboards, radio, television, magazines, and newspapers. Many newsagents, corner stores and supermarkets entice you with a discounted chocolate bar purchase at the checkout point. Food store layouts ensure that sweets and treats are highly visible both at the entrance and exit in addition to the multiple aisles inside which stock an inconceivable quantity and variety of non-essential, sugar-laden food items. This type of product placement is difficult to resist when you have had a tough day and feel like you 'want to be a little naughty', 'need to treat yourself', or 'live a little because life is too short to say no all the time'.

**Table 20.** Dessert and snack phrases

| | |
|---|---|
| "Life is uncertain. Eat dessert first" | Ernestine Ulmer |
| "Cookies are made of butter and love" | Norwegian Proverb |
| "Seize the moment. Remember all those women on the Titanic who waved off the dessert cart" | Erma Bombeck |
| "Desserts are the fairy tales of the kitchen - a happily-ever-after to supper" | Terri Guillemets |
| "A balanced diet is a cookie in each hand" | Unknown |
| "A party without a cake is just a meeting" | Julia Child |

As you are already aware, traditional desserts are never an essential part of optimum nutrition nor were they historically served on a daily basis. Modern-day food abundance is in stark contrast to chronicled times of food scarcity. If you feel that you *need* a dessert after your meals then the problem can be twofold. Desserts can perceivably meet our emotional needs and this promotes bad eating habits rather than provide essential nutrients. The second consideration is that your main meal may be lacking in key nutrients that promote satiety, that state of being where you have met your nutritional needs. Provided that you have eaten enough food, the issue might be that you omitted to add essential fats to your meal such as a serving of avocado, olives, oily fish, or oils like extra virgin olive, walnut, flaxseed, or hemp seed. Address these omissions before you convince yourself that you need a treat after your main meals on a regular basis.

Different cultures have different attitudes towards desserts. Some have learnt to nurture the belief that a dessert should contain substantial calories count consisting of sugar, cream and butter. Others view dessert as a mere conclusion of a meal enjoyed with loved ones, consisting of a modest piece of cheese, fruit, or yoghurt, a cup of tea, coffee, or even a digestive aid in the form of an alcoholic beverage (Cognac or whiskey). Perhaps your best approach to settling the dessert debate is to consider the 'Naturally Slender Eating Strategy' developed by Connirae and Steve Andreas. The crux of their strategy is to imagine how choosing a certain food will make you feel as it passes through your digestive tract. Will it sit well in your stomach (gut) after you have enjoyed it or will you experience undesirable symptoms a few hours later? Are you choosing a dessert merely based on the immediate sensation of pleasure without any thought for the long-term consequences? As an adult, you will have had many repeated experiences in your past and it should be easy to recall how certain dessert options made you feel. If you engage in this process every time, the option of post-meal dessert arises and you come to the conclusion that there will be no regrettable side-effects then, dear reader, enjoy your dessert. Even though sweet, calorie dense desserts can never be promoted as part of an essential nutrient-dense diet, the choice to indulge and treat yourself to a guilty pleasure is yours, and only yours to make.

But what about healthy desserts? Health food bloggers are flooding the internet with guilt-free desserts and treats such as mini strawberry cheesecake. This delight consists of coconut palm sugar, fat-free cream cheese, low-fat yoghurt, strawberries, dates, almonds, and a few other ingredients. A serving is stated to contain 22 g of sugar (almost 6 teaspoons), which is just a fraction less than 1 part of a Mars® Duo Chocolate bar (25.4 g). Sugar content aside, if you crave strawberries then a few freshly picked berries should be enough to satisfy your yearning after a well-constructed main meal. Perhaps a healthy vegan avocado chocolate dessert captures your fancy. The ingredients typically include avocado, cocoa powder, almond milk, maple syrup, with fruit to garnish. To adhere to the ideal plate composition why not rather add avocado to your main meal and eat either a modest piece of dark chocolate or fresh fruit if you have to satisfy your hankering for dessert. My clinical observation is that patients too often opt to reduce their food intake because dessert is desired.

Whether the recipe says healthy, guilt-free, sugar-free, or fat-free, a dessert remains a non-essential option. The choice to conclude your meals with any one of these or a more traditional offering will always be yours to make. Be informed and choose wisely.

## How Can You Incorporate Change in Practical Terms?

Now you are ready for a step-by-step action plan to help you achieve optimum nutrition:

1. Unpack all your food and snack cupboards and drawers and take stock of what stares back at you,
2. Group the food into protein, carbohydrates, fats, dairy, sugar snacks and sweets, savoury snacks, sauces and condiments,
3. Get rid of all the non-essential options including treats. It is easier to desire something when it is available and more difficult when you have to go out and source these empty calories,
4. Make a shopping list based on the nutrient-dense options listed above and plan a trip to your store or food supplier of choice,
5. Once you get home after sourcing good food options, wash the fresh produce, let it dry, and store in airtight containers in the fridge or leave vegetables such as potatoes, sweet potatoes, beetroots, and avocados in a dark, dry cupboard or larder,
6. Arrange your fridge such that the various vegetables are the first thing you see when you open the fridge door,
7. Store cereals and grains in airtight containers in a dark, dry cupboard or larder,
8. Place oils, such as olive, walnut, sesame seed, or avocado in a dark, dry cupboard or larder. Coconut oil can be stored in the fridge as it is already in a solid state at room temperature,

9. Nuts and seeds are also best stored in the fridge. I use clean glass jars as inexpensive storage containers. This allows you to see the various options without needing to use labels,

10. When preparing a meal, or a snack (which should ideally just be a mini version of a meal), first choose a protein option. Remember that we want to maximise our plant-based food options so look for nuts, seeds, legumes, and beans first. When you do choose an animal product, be mindful to choose an ethically sourced option that is not pre-prepared i.e. a salmon fillet is a better option than a store prepared fish cake and similarly a small piece of beef in place of a pre-prepared crusty steak and ale pie. There are innumerable recipe books, magazines, videos, and blogs which can show you how to prepare protein options and by spending time experimenting in the kitchen you will soon become your own expert. Refrain from deep frying your food and opt for grilling and oven baking instead. Many options such as nuts, seeds, and hummus require no cooking and neither do tinned sardines, tuna, smoked salmon and mackerel,

11. Now find at least two different vegetables to turn into a salad, lightly steam, stir-fry, grill, or cook to resemble a stew or soup. Your first option should ideally be vegetables that you can eat raw such as avocados, fresh tomatoes, lettuce, carrots, and cucumber. Leave the starchy vegetables (sweet potatoes, corn, turnips, and Swedes) for when you choose your carbohydrate-rich part of the meal,

12. The next ingredient is your cereal or grain option. Open the relevant cupboard or walk to the larder and choose a desirable option. Here the first option should be a naturally gluten-free choice, such as rice, potatoes, starchy vegetables, polenta (ground maize), quinoa, sorghum, and buckwheat. I re-emphasise, gluten is not an issue for *everybody*, however, it is a common ingredient used in restaurants, cafes, and street food outlets and therefore a little trickier to avoid when you are eating away from home or ordering takeout meals.

Your best strategy, in terms of ensuring greater dietary diversity, is to choose a gluten-free option when you are in charge of preparing meals,

13. The last ingredient to add is an essential fat. Even if you have chosen an avocado, nuts or seeds as one of your meal ingredients, adding an oil, such as olive, walnut, or flaxseed to your salad or cooked vegetables completes your basic nutrient requirements. This essential addition promotes satiety and reduces the feeling that you are lacking something,

14. Call the family or other dining companions, sit around a table, take a moment to enjoy the aroma wafting from your plate, and enjoy every mouthful whilst discussing the day's events or reminiscing over other non-confrontational topics. Ideally, we want the dining experience to be stress-free, relaxed, and a social affair,

15. Note that you have just satisfied your nutritional needs in an enjoyable fashion whilst being in the company of loved ones or at peace with your own company,

16. Be thankful that you are alive and nourished.

## Hedonistic Dining: Reconciling Festive Eating with Optimum Nutrition

It seems that before I can adequately recuperate from one celebration another festive holiday appears on the horizon. I get the feeling that Christmas decorations and music are thrust upon us earlier than seems socially acceptable with increasing anticipation every year. We have just managed to pick up the firework debris from the garden after the recent Guy Fawkes celebration, or Thanksgiving when Christmas and year-end decorations suddenly sprout up in most public places. Major shopping destinations, such as Oxford Street in London, brim with festive cheer and illuminating decorations overhanging this long stretch of commercial heaven before we formally say goodbye to summer fruits and hello to hot chocolate and hearty soups.

Traditional British Christmas and American Thanksgiving meals can be heavy and require ample preparation leaving the host(ess) rather worse for wear before the meal even begins. Around about the time when the warm custard is poured over the Christmas pudding or the cream whipped for the pumpkin pie is when most people plan their New Year's resolutions, often focusing on weight management. Obviously, the implementation of weight reducing strategies can only realistically come into play once the New Year has been welcomed with appropriately traditional and excessive consumption of alcohol. Those ever-present New Year's resolutions and good intentions include the popular decision to lose the excess weight in the shortest time possible so that we can be ready for Valentine's Day romantic meal for two.

Given your newly acquired nutritional knowledge, you can minimise the calorific after-effect of traditional year-end, and other traditional indulgent dining experiences, by making a couple of easy to incorporate culinary tweaks:

1.  Start your festive day with a protein dense breakfast. This can include scrambled eggs or an omelette with chopped tomatoes, red pepper, and even some smoked salmon, hummus, or bacon. A thin slice of toast can be added, but is best avoided because you are inevitably going to be presented with a buffet of starchy options at the main event,

2.  Instead of coffee at breakfast, enjoy green tea or a herbal alternative to ensure you stay well hydrated as alcohol is probably going to feature at some point later on in the day. Alcohol has a dehydrating effect and adds to your liver's workload. Silvia's story showed how your liver has important work to do with regards to cholesterol and we have all seen the alarming news regarding high cholesterol and cardiovascular disease,

3.  The roast turkey, duck, goose, salmon, ham, lamb or nut loaf will undoubtedly be the centrepiece accompanied by ample roast potatoes. To lessen the calorific load (and ease inevitable abdominal bloating), choose lightly steamed broccoli or spinach and grated carrot salad topped with pine nuts and cherry tomatoes as an accompaniment. One of my personal favourites is raw fennel with fresh orange slices,

4.  Add a jug or bottle of plain or sparkling water on the table to lessen the alcohol or soft drink load, which inevitably adds to abdominal discomfort,
5.  A gentle stroll in a nearby park or just around the block after your festive meal allows for some digestive relief, not necessarily achieved by sitting down on the sofa straight away,
6.  A light soup or salad topped with leftover protein at least 3 hours before retiring to bed for the night may be the answer to lessen abdominal discomfort, which can exacerbate sleep disturbances.

At this point in the book, you are aware that optimal digestion is best achieved when not stressed. Therefore, ensure that your dining companions are well chosen and that the workload is well delegated. Most people appreciate the hard work that accompanies a meal for many guests and will not, on this special day, refuse your request to help clear the table, load the dishwasher or use a tea towel to dry the dishes.

Focus on your well-prepared meal and be thankful that you survived yet another festive meal without major incident.

## Eating Out

There are so many eateries dotted around the globe that it is difficult not to be able or at least tempted to eat out. You might prefer to dine out of the house due to time constraints or perhaps mere convenience. The privilege of working close to home and being able to nip back for lunch is only available to a select few people. And even if you work from home, you might want a change of scenery and a bit of company every now and then and enjoy a meal prepared by a professional cook or celebrated chef. You might even need to replenish your dwindling food supply but prefer to dine out rather than head to a supermarket to stock up. Your family might prefer a Friday night takeout rather than a home cooked meal because it creates a more social environment in line with starting the much anticipated weekend. Whatever the motivation, eating out has become a part of life.

I eat out often and it is already ingrained in me to follow the ideal plate composition. That means that there are many eateries that I avoid because I know it will be very difficult to order a meal consisting of a variety of vegetables. Remember that half a plate of vegetables is a very important part of the ideal plate composition. I have heard some very vocal authors say, what you do once can surely not be that bad for you and if you worry about what food will be served you probably have a food issue. Based on that criteria I have a food issue.

My food concerns are based around the premise that I do not eat food purely because it is edible. I have three square meals per day and not only do I want to enjoy the taste and social aspect of eating, I want my chosen food options to be nutritious. I view it as an inexpensive insurance policy against preventable ails. Much like heart disease patients are prescribed an aspirin a day to prevent the formation of clots which might trigger a heart attack or a stroke. It is accepted that an aspirin will not be 100% effective for every patient and similarly, my food choices may not protect me completely against every ailment, all of the time. I believe that it is worth minimising my risk and at the same time maximising my enjoyment of food.

When it comes to certain food options I choose not to partake. I have no desire to eat a highly processed meat-like option which lists dubious ingredients on the package, even though everybody else at an event chooses to. Nor would I choose to partake in a social event where all the revellers imbibe in excessive alcohol to have a good time. There are instances where you might find it difficult to gauge what is in the food that is being served. The horse meat scandal in the UK in 2013 showed that even if you study every food label, that list might not be a true reflection of what a food product actually contains. The relatively frequent outbreaks of food poisoning following unsafe food preparation practices or unsuspected infected food choices make me consider my participation in certain social events very carefully. In my opinion, even one bout of traveller's diarrhoea is one too many.

Even when it comes to treats and desserts, I have my favourites which I will sometimes indulge in, but I will not eat every biscuit, sweet, or pastry that some kind host or work colleague offers me, just to be polite. And despite the many advertisements that show me how delicious and nutritious milk is, I do not add it to my tea or coffee because I prefer the taste of my hot beverages without it. No matter how tough my day is, I do not need a cup of sweetened tea to pick me up because I, quite simply, dislike sugar in my drinks. These are a few of my personal preferences that have changed and developed over years. They have little to do with showing how 'good' I am and are solely based on my own unique predilection.

Religious views, moral objections, personal likes and dislikes not only determine what food you buy but which restaurant you will choose and what dish you are likely to order.

For someone to suggest that you have a food issue when we all follow our own set of preferences is rather misguided. Setting aside those criteria, it is possible to follow the ideal plate composition even when dining out, provided that you research your options carefully and plan ahead.

## How Can I Eat out and Follow the Ideal Plate Composition?

When ordering food in a restaurant or take-away facility your focus is to look for a good source of protein, be it tofu, legumes, eggs, fish, or meat. Then you should try to find a selection of vegetables, either the choice of the day or a generous side salad. Lastly, choose the carbohydrate or starch option that takes your fancy, something like new potatoes, rice, bread, or fries.

When your plate arrives it might represent any of the following:
- ✓ Tofu and vegetable stir-fry with a side order of noodles or rice,
- ✓ Quinoa salad, which might include edamame beans, string beans, spinach, and tomato,
- ✓ Hummus, lettuce, tomato and avocado on multigrain bread,
- ✓ Bean and vegetable wrap (burrito),
- ✓ Scrambled eggs with smoked salmon on rye with spinach and fresh tomatoes,
- ✓ Egg omelette on rye with bell pepper, avocado and tomato,

- ✓ Egg, bacon, mushroom, tomato, and spinach with a slice of wholemeal bread,
- ✓ Lentil and vegetable soup with a small bread roll,
- ✓ Grilled salmon with mixed green salad and a few new potatoes,
- ✓ Grilled mackerel or sardines with fries and a generous side salad,
- ✓ Chicken and vegetable soup with a small bread roll,
- ✓ Steak with potato, sweet potato or polenta fries and a generous side salad,
- ✓ Lamb curry with mixed vegetables and a side order of rice,
- ✓ Crispy duck with mixed vegetables and a side order of egg fried rice.

Given the wonderful array of eateries in most towns and cities, it is possible to find food that is made in line with the ideal plate composition.

## How Do People Feel About Changing Their Diet?

Many of my patients have agreed to share their feelings around changing their diet. Their experiences might help you understand how addressing their own unique food choices impacted on them. If you have explored certain dietary changes motivated by the media, friends or family, you might find that your journey echoes some of their thoughts. A select few phrases might even motivate you to take that very first step towards improved health if you have been considering it for some time.

I ultimately include these observations to help you see that adopting the ideal plate composition makes optimum health achievable for people of all walks of life, people like you.

"I can imagine it might be difficult for people who have never done something like this before. I was very gung-ho about it and very optimistic but in all honesty, after so many years of implementing changes and holistic regimens, I was getting extremely frustrated when I would have temporary results and continue to get extremely ill. People can't give up if they really want to heal. It can happen overnight and it can also be a very, very, very long road." – Brooke

"I'm not sure that I acted immediately upon your advice although I could see the connection between my 'depressed' lifestyle and the need to eat more healthily." – Michael

"I felt good about changing my diet, extremely positive about the recommendations and they were clear and easy to follow. Regarding the recommendations I felt that the food changes and suggestions were excellent, and I have for the most part maintained this." – Rachel

"I felt extremely worried about my nutrition and my energy levels and felt like I needed re-educating about nutrition and food choices. Once I got my head around what I should be eating and what to avoid it was easy to apply the changes." – Charlotte

"Deep down inside I knew that we are what we eat – so cakes, crisps and ready meals weren't great. But until you look at your food squarely in the face and ask what it's doing to benefit you or doing against you it doesn't really sink in. You made me look at my food squarely in the face, and once I'd done that, and seen the results of changing what I was eating there really was no going back. I was ready and desperate for it. I think if someone wasn't ready to make the change in their life then they'd find it hard. I felt guided and supported by your knowledge, and a bit like I was a co-creator in an experiment. Remember you may have done this a million times, but to each new patient, the protocol is an experiment. The changes themselves were strict and precise but I didn't find them hard – because I was ready to solve my health problem and knew that I was ultimately responsible for any change. I think that might be the crux of it. I knew I had to make the changes for it be effective, I didn't expect a tablet, a drug, an operation or anything else done to me or for me to heal me." – Shez

"I was very enthusiastic at the start and could really see the benefit. I had wondered why I had felt the way that I had for a long time and the advice really helped. To begin with, it wasn't too difficult but I have a very busy and stressful job and find that 'comfort food' which is usually not the most healthy is a way of coping with this. So I swing up and down with weight and ability to eat the way that I'd like to. I find I am either 'in a zone' where I am able to manage what I eat effectively and feel good or I am out of the zone and crave carbs and sugar. There seems very little middle ground which is dispiriting." – Liz

"I found it challenging, but was committed to doing it for the long-term gain." – Steve

"I was fully prepared to do whatever it took to improve my health. At the time, I had been signed off work for more than a month, with a chest infection and then post-viral fatigue (which subsequently was diagnosed as chronic fatigue/M.E.) and I was desperate to get well enough to go back to work and my life. So when Wilma gave me a diet plan I followed it 100%." – Haifa

"When I initially went to see Wilma, I was already following an anti-candida diet but was still experiencing symptoms of fatigue, brain fogginess and digestive issues. Wilma suggested some testing which would show if candida was present. This was money well spent as the results showed I did not have candida BUT what I did have was extremely poor good bacteria, which made total sense to me. Wilma prescribed a good food regime and dietary supplements, which helped immensely." – Anne

"I was happy to make changes to diet as I was desperate to get better." – Martha

"I felt excited to change my diet as you gave me really great ideas about how to introduce foods … I still make huge salads now with most meals as I too am a lazy cook." – Catherine

"I felt positive and looking forward to it as I believed that it would make a difference." – Nuno

"I was very happy and excited to start the super free diet that you recommended. I was suffering badly from recurrent thrush and desperate to do anything to improve my condition." – Maryan

"I had tried lots of different excluding diets before but always felt that they were extremely strict and very hard to stick to. I wasn't nervous about changing my diet because I had done it so many times before but this time I felt a lot more positive about the diet alongside the natural supplements. After speaking with you I finally felt like you understood how I was feeling and knew what would help so felt confident giving it a go. I was also glad that you didn't tell me it was just 'IBS' like every other person did!" – Emily

"At first I felt quite daunted by a lot of it and felt as if I was missing out on a normal life and that my condition had made me feel as if I could no longer enjoy food. Nutrition and good mental health work together and that realisation made me experience significant health improvements." – Jane

"I was happy to make changes as I was already doing of some of them before being asked. This did not seem to be a major change for me. However, further discipline was needed to be consistent." – Sunny

"I found it quite daunting at first, there was a lot of information to take in and many changes to make. It was a challenging few months but I have learnt a lot. I am now much more aware of the food and drink I am putting into my body. I have a new perspective which will benefit me for the future." – Natalie

"Wilma Kirsten looked at all my symptoms holistically and was able to explain in great detail what was happening within my body and how my diet affects this. This knowledge gave me the motivation to stick to my new diet." – Elwira

"I couldn't wait to change my diet as the guidelines were easy, with a wide range of foods and diversity being the key rather than restriction and elimination diets I had been suggested before, and to no avail. I liked that I was given a list of foods to eat, rather than to avoid like other nutritionists had given me. I also liked the portion suggestions or half a plate of veg/greens etc. as this was visual and easy to do. I felt encouraged by the diversity of foods I was supposed to eat as I had always been scared of what foods I shouldn't be eating before. Also, they weren't ridiculous suggestions that you could only get in a certain health shop, they were just wholesome, affordable foods. I focused on what I could eat rather than what I couldn't." – Francesca

"I was very willing to change my diet in line with your recommendations, firstly because you were the only practitioner that was able to give me direction after years of endless doctors' appointments and being treated like a guinea pig with medications that only made my symptoms worse and caused other health problems. Secondly, you did not only advise changes but you explained to me the benefits and how certain foods have either a positive or negative impact in regards to my health condition." – Kaouthar

## What Are the Benefits of Changing Your Diet?

All journeys come with certain challenges, least of all the ones that make you re-evaluate your long-standing eating behaviour. You may not have viewed your eating patterns as overtly problematic but a seed of intrigue has been planted. After reading the stories in chapter one to eight you might now be thinking that it is worth exploring alternative meal choices but you could be wondering if it will benefit you in the end. To help you understand what is involved in changing your diet in line with the ideal plate composition and what you could gain from these changes, I include feedback from an array of my patients. These faced similar life challenges to you and have had comparable reservations at the start of their individual health journeys. I shall let their words help you make an informed decision.

"I am now doing incredibly well and I will also say that most of it is mental. I still have my days where I eat and drink things I 'should not' but for the most part I follow the same diet that we worked with and I am on very minimal supplementation through a healer/acupuncturist. I would say that because people have the power to change their diets, it is a great place to start. It is tangible and visual and you can track your progress that way. But I don't think everything is about the food and the supplements, obviously, we know that. But starting with diet starts to create shifts and opens up new doors. I believe most healing happens by taking back your power. And if you need to be on a diet to realise you have some control, so be it. It also happens that eating healthily feels good but the benefits of taking action for yourself is what really makes a difference." – Brooke

"I was given the tools to proceed in a proactive and comprehensive manner. The results were swift and substantial in terms of my energy levels, general health and moving towards a healthier weight. This had a long-lasting and very positive impact on my life." – Mark

"I have benefited greatly from changing my diet. I have been losing weight slowly but consistently over the last 3–4 years. I still have a way to go but at my heaviest, I was 210 pounds and I am now 170. Sadly, my PMDD was far too severe to cure through lifestyle changes alone. It got to the stage where I could no longer function for half the month and my life was so bad I wanted to die. It required surgery and so 2 years ago I had one ovary removed. The improvement was immediate. Since then I have had nearly no or very mild PMS and easier periods. When I tried a progesterone pill it sent me crazy indicating, I believe, that there is an innate problem in my body's ability to cope with hormonal fluctuations which were too severe to be influenced by diet. (Literally, the removal of an ovary has completely stopped the panic attacks, binge eating, paranoia, serious depression, inability to drive, suicidal thoughts). I was going to have a hysterectomy but I suggested one ovary and they agreed. With regards to the adrenal fatigue, I also needed to change my lifestyle significantly to fully combat it. Two years ago, I became very ill with constant tonsillitis and shingles and my doc just said I was over exhausted so I moved schools, taught part-time and do other little jobs, meaning I can focus more on my exercise and nutrition. So, I benefited a lot from the recommendations and have enjoyed implementing them and 'retraining myself' but ultimately my health problems required more drastic measures to improve them!" – Rachel

"Once I got my head around what I should be eating and what to avoid it was easy to apply the changes. I benefited greatly from the dietary advice and felt the vitamins improved my energy levels as well as the food." – Charlotte

"It was easy once I realised it was about creating new habits. Morning routine, evening routine, shopping routine, time for a treat routine. These things didn't go away they just had to be changed. Eczema improved short term, my skin improved long term. But when I have had a relapse (whilst on holiday drinking lots of wine and eating lots of bread) I've been able to see clearly what's caused it, and that through my choices I'm responsible for it, and I been able to coax my skin back to a place of calm.

Once I made the changes, I soon realised how much of an effect sugar and simple carbohydrates had been having on my brain and mood. I feel a lot more present and less 'drugged' with less sugar in my life.

My views on the importance of nutrition and what good nutrition is have changed dramatically. We were comfortably off and busy so ready meals where the norm in our house. We were already vegetarian but we ate a lot of vegetarian ready meals and a lot of cheese, and bread. Now we shop for raw materials, organic when possible and make what we're going to eat. We seldom eat bread and try to avoid dairy. We've learnt that processed is poor nutrition and more processed the poorer.

And finally, to start with I had no real opinion on the value of nutritional therapists, now I recommend it as a starting point for people with any allergy or gut problem." – Shez

"When I stick to what I should be doing I do feel much better but that is way easier said than done and quick fixes for feeling better in a day are often more attractive than long-term healthy eating!" – Liz

"Some; cutting down caffeine fine and alcohol too, dairy harder and sugar the hardest to get my taste buds around. I think I never did it totally properly instead just cut down on all these hugely. Gave up caffeine in total. I had rest at the same time too so hard to gauge but the results you did showed that my adrenals were better. And I'm glad to have more food awareness – even if I have mostly gone back to my old ways. I'm more conscious of the decisions I make and the impact the food could have." – Wendy

"It was hard! I saw a marked improvement to my asthma to a point where I didn't really need any medication any more, although I was not able to sustain this and it did not improve my primary condition which was my chronic cough." – Steve

"It wasn't that hard for me to implement the changes to my diet as I was committed to doing so and am naturally very disciplined! Also, my family were very accommodating and supportive of my dietary changes. The dietary changes and supplementation were crucial to my improved health outcome. The biggest surprise was the impact it had on other areas of my health – after one month on Wilma's programme I experienced no PMS for the first time in my life – until then I hadn't realised that hormonal health was so closely linked to nutrition.

I know for sure that without changing my diet and healing my gut there is no way that my recovery from chronic ill health would have been possible. Years of stress, poor nutrition, undiagnosed food intolerances and antibiotics had wreaked havoc on my body and to this day, I pay close attention to my diet. Once you realise how fundamental nutrition is to overall health, there is no going back!" – Haifa

"I didn't find the changes too difficult considering I was already changing my diet prior to our appointment, but the recommendations from Wilma were easy to put into practice and to follow on a daily basis. The only change I did not make, probably because I didn't realise how important it was, was to stop dairy. This is something I have recently put into practice and I can already feel the benefits, with less bloating.

I have benefited hugely from the additional changes and ensure I keep as much as possible to the plan. If I don't I start to experience the symptoms again, although not to the same extent. Getting back onto the healthy eating stops the symptoms. I do believe this is a lifelong change, and I feel so much better and have much more awareness than I did prior to seeing Wilma. To be honest, in reference to the diet I was already following the healthy eating as you know. What did specifically make a difference to my health were the supplements you suggested especially the magnesium, vitamin D, the CQ30 and the oil of oregano. I still use them now." – Anne

"It was harder than I thought to incorporate changes as yeast extract is in pretty much everything. However, I learnt a great deal about new foods and new ways of eating and as a result, although I now have been back to yeast sugar etc. I have incorporated new ingredients and the experienced made me discover new foods and see nutrition in a new way." – Martha

"I had to re-think my diet and eating habits to follow your advice, which was quite challenging but also fun. The changes cured me for about 6 months, after which I think marriage and work stress dragged me down again. However, my other condition of ankylosing spondylitis went away when I adopted this diet and, as I have stayed on it, has not returned!" – Ted

189

"I wouldn't say it was hard but more a different mindset. I had to make myself a priority and organise my meals a day in advance, as opposed to skipping lunch then eating crisps and chocolate mid-afternoon. For the time I did it, I felt really positive and empowered. I definitely noticed my mood improved and the best benefit was having more energy during the daytime." – Catherine

"I would say the changes were not easy but definitely achievable with some guidance. I benefited by regaining some of the energy that I had lost and also the fact that I started to eat in a healthier way which can only benefit me in the future." – Nuno

"I found the diet easy enough as I could eat a whole lot of vegetables and meat and poultry and fish and nuts. It only needed a lot of planning and preparation in advance to be able to stick with it and not end up eating something unsuitable. I would like to mention that I had sugar craving from time to time. And after two months of dieting when I stopped I did suffer a bit from sugar craving. I think it is best not to go back to normal diet straight away. And best to start introducing carbohydrates and sugar little by little.

I felt very good, a lot of energy. My asthma and congestion improved dramatically. In a way that I did not need to use any medication while I was on this diet. Unfortunately, the problem I had with thrush did not disappear. I did get better and the condition improved. But I still had to take medication and I still suffered in a milder version until I stopped tamoxifen. However, I believe the diet and your recommendations helped me a lot to improve my health and body so when I stopped tamoxifen I was in a strong place to overcome my illness." – Maryan

"I didn't find it as hard as I thought, I was also in university at the time. I think because I was so determined and after trying so many different things I really wanted to give this a good go. I always made easy meals that didn't take too much time. The hardest thing was going out for meals/drinks with friends. However, due to the immediate benefits I felt from the beginning, it didn't bother me too much not being able to have certain things because I felt better for not having it. Also, I knew that the diet was just more strict to start with whilst taking the supplements alongside it. I always remember it had just been two days since I had started the diet and the changes were already so apparent. This then made me want to continue the diet and I did so for 10 weeks alongside the supplements and I have never felt better. I felt like I was really healing my body. Finally, my symptoms of bloating and constipation had improved significantly and I had so much more energy! I started to really look forward to eating nutritious meals just knowing the benefits they were going to have. Not only that, I finally knew what types of foods affected my stomach in a bad way, so I could choose to take it or leave it. I also learnt about the incredible importance of eating plenty of fruit and veg!" – Emily

"I found changing my diet hard at first as living with a partner who doesn't understand the condition made this difficult to change. Although diet played a large part in my condition I felt it wasn't specific enough for my training requirements. At my gym, I have a nutritionist who understands adrenal conditions and so he advised some supplements such as whey protein that helped immensely. Most of my health issues were related to several toxic relationships and since splitting with my partner I have started to feel a little better. In conclusion, I think that nutrition and good mental health working together has been what has made me start to recover." – Jane

"Easy as these were in line with my values and I could see the benefits on my health even if it did not directly cure my issues. Changes were slow but I could see the benefits within a few months with my condition improving." – Sunny

"I found the diet very tough at the start, it was difficult to resist sugary foods and dairy products. However, I was determined to stick with it and as the weeks went on it became easier. The diet involved a great deal of planning and organisation as I had to prepare most of my meals and snacks each day in advance. At first, this was a chore and rather time-consuming, however, it has now become a way of life and it ensures I eat filling and nutritious meals, free from unnecessary sugars and additives regularly throughout the day. It has been a very rewarding journey. After around 6–8 weeks I began to have more good days without any of the nasty symptoms, the bloating also reduced significantly so this motivated me to continue with the diet. I have learnt a lot about food and dietary requirements along the way. It has been really interesting and useful." – Natalie

"The change was easy as I was given a lot of delicious alternatives to my usual products, list of products I can and cannot eat. For years, I was struggling every day with a variety of symptoms, from headaches to bloating after almost every meal and recurring infections in my body. The supplements and diet have helped immensely with that. On top of the lack of my previous symptoms, I have to mention the psychological benefits of the diet. Years of headaches bring you down, I forgot how I felt before. Now I am myself again thanks to the changes advised by Wilma Kirsten." – Elwira

"Very easy as long as I prepared my lunches for work. I am a terrible cook but they weren't bizarre recipes, just the simplest type of food that you can get in any supermarket. I just picked off the list for each night and my partner ate the same. My whole life turned around; I was no longer in pain, the awful taste in my mouth subsided, I lost weight, I stopped getting bladder infections, my allergy symptoms improved, I felt happier and more energised. I basically got my life back. I had been trying for years to get better and spent thousands of pounds, to no avail, until I found Wilma Kirsten. I don't think I could have carried on feeling the way I was before I got better." – Francesca

"Excluding sugar from my diet was extremely hard but it did teach me a new way of eating, so that was extremely helpful." – Nurshen

"I felt it was very simple to implement those changes providing I spent a little time thinking ahead and planning my meals as it's very easy to choose a non-beneficial option out of laziness. The dietary changes benefited me hugely. Previously, I had been suffering from severe heartburn and acid reflux for so long. I remember waking up in the early hours of the morning feeling like my stomach was burning and I would have to get out of bed to eat as food seemed to suppress the burning sensation for all of a few hours. And then I would feel the burning once again and stuff myself with food. I spent every day worrying about having food on hand just so I could get a little relief from the burning sensation. My life became a nightmare until Wilma advised me in regards with food that I was continuously consuming that was actually making the problem worse. She advised me on what I should be eating to eliminate the problem and yes, it worked! After years of constantly taking different medications prescribed by GP's that never actually worked and ended up causing more harm. Thank you very much, Wilma, because I have not had any heartburn, acid reflux, or burning in my stomach since! I would like to add that Wilma is the only practitioner that genuinely gave me the time and answered my questions and talked about my concerns with me. She always responded to me no matter how busy she was and spent time either talking to me on the phone or replying to each and every email I sent. All without charging extra! Every other practitioner charged a fee even to respond to email questions. Wilma, you truly are a lovely and very honest lady." – Kaouthar

# Final Thoughts

## My Story

The Dalai Lama, when asked what surprised him most about humanity, answered:

*Man. Because he sacrifices his health in order to make money. Then he sacrifices money to recuperate his health. And then he is so anxious about the future that he does not enjoy the present; the result being that he does not live in the present or the future; he lives as if he is never going to die, and then he dies having never really lived.*

For those of you who are wondering about my heritage, I am South African. Born and raised in a conservative Afrikaans (Dutch colonist) home. That means meat was plentiful and meals were always a family affair.

My first bad food memory was when I was 3, being looked after by a traditional African nanny who made me maize meal (pap) with tomato and onion sauce. I hated onions and proceeded to empty the contents of my toddler appropriate bowl in my mother's pride geranium bush. For my efforts, my bottom was tinted red by a slipper. Where I come from, you do not waste food.

My biggest culinary challenge came when I fell in love with an Italian and married him on my $22^{nd}$ birthday. That cross-cultural marriage introduced me to food never seen or sampled before and required an open mind and a very adventurous palate. All of which came to me very slowly.

Where the Italian influence introduced me to rabbit, quails (I still remember lifting the pot's lid and being horrified by the sight of those dead little birds), fresh homemade pasta, and salads with every meal, I brought some questionable dishes to

194

the table. The first meal I presented my husband with was a roast chicken, which I drowned in pure butter. That poor chicken was both smothered and roasted beyond all acceptable culinary requirements.

I learnt early on in our courtship that serving an Italian a mock Italian meal is a cardinal sin. In South Africa, pasta only reached our shores in the late 90s and was considered an avoidable foreign food. I was blissfully unaware that serving a boil-pasta-in-a-bag meal for my husband was not the way to his heart.

Years later, my whole family decided to adopt a vegan (strict vegetarian) diet. For those of you who are not familiar with the term vegan, that means avoiding any food that is vaguely animal related, be it meat, fish, eggs, milk, cheese, butter, and honey. This is not only a way of eating that requires some organisation, it can completely void your social calendar, except for those very dear friends who, despite your awkwardness, still want to entertain you. The first incidence was when my friend presented us with a feast of a meal that tingled the taste buds and had us line up for seconds. Upon closer inspection, we discovered bacon in every dish.

On another occasion, we were invited to dinner by a lady who had a vegetable garden rivalling Raymond Blanc's Le Manoir Aux Quat'Saison in Great Milton, Oxford. She had certainly walked more than the extra mile in preparing a meal to write home about. The only problem was that the starter of rice parcels hid shrimp inside. The ethos of a vegan diet is clearly not that well understood by people who themselves do not follow this way of eating. Even though the bacon bits and shrimp had no ill effects on my health, it was just a little unexpected.

During the few years of following a vegan diet, we spent time in Tokyo where sushi and sashimi reign supreme. Husband had a colleague print business cards explaining our food preferences and we presented that at every restaurant or eatery we frequented as the language was clearly an obstacle. Did any of the chefs sneak in anything that was not on our list? I am sure they did. Did we enjoy our food? You bet. The best experience in Japan was when we decided to visit Kamakura. After getting lost in the woods, as you do in a country where you neither speak the language nor are able to read the road signs, we stumbled upon a Buddhist restaurant. Buddhist cuisine is predominantly vegetarian and this particular vegan eatery also had presentation down to perfection. Every dish was a visual marvel and the gustatory experience was sublime. No dining experience would be without a faux pas or two for me and I managed to offend the locals by blowing my nose in public.

So what do I do for a living? I am a nutrition consultant who likes to challenge the 5-a-day message to be more in line with the WHO recommendations of 10–14 portions of fruit and vegetables a day. What do I look for in a meal? The most important ingredient on my plate has to be some form of recognisable vegetable. I have been known to demand a salad at many an eatery who do not normally serve it. Whether chefs deliver it with a dusting of disbelief is another question. My philosophy is, if I can pick, fish, or shoot it (figuratively speaking), then I will happily tuck in. I can pick a broccoli, but not a quiche Lorraine. I can fish a fish, but not a fish cake. I can shoot a lamb, but I cannot shoot a Shepherd's pie. Clearly, if I am to select the raw ingredients and assemble my own quiche, pie or fish creation, then all is in line with my nutritional philosophy.

I now follow an all-inclusive diet meaning I enjoy a vegan stir fry as much as I do a venison stew. I buy as many artichokes as I do zucchini (courgettes) depending on the season and availability. My code of conduct starts with meal planning, followed by purchasing the individual ingredients, preparing it at home, presenting the final product at a dining room or kitchen table to my dining compatriots, ensuring that it aims to please all the senses, and ultimately promotes long-term health.

We all have our personal likes and dislikes and my preference is always for food that I can recognise. I love fresh tomatoes but not tomato sauce meant for potato fries. I thoroughly enjoy grilled mackerel but am less eager to sample a fish cake. I am transported to culinary heaven by a leafy salad with a good measure of extra virgin olive oil, but will politely refuse any other salad dressing. If the food label leaves me perplexed then I would rather avoid that particular offering. If someone lovingly prepared a meal, I shall tuck in with gusto. And if a host is an avid baker then I might indulge a little. I am, however, not easily tempted by cakes and desserts that have a long shelf life. Nor are my taste buds tingled by a roast drowned in gravy.

Woody Allen is reported to have said,

*I will not eat oysters. I want my food dead. Not sick. Not wounded. Dead.*

So who comes to see me? If you have been given Omeprazole, Amytriptyline and even Colpermin and you still double up with abdominal pain or embarrassingly let out one offensive wind too many, then I am the door you knock on. If you have been given the oral contraceptive for acne, then had the Mirena coil inserted to balance your hormones and you still feel the urge to strangle your nearest and dearest two weeks out of four, my clinic is the one you should come to. If stress is interfering with your sleep and libido, I can help. In a nutshell, I see people who have tried everything and are still feeling stressed, tired, bothered, bloated, congested, pre-menstrual, and generally unwell without apparent rhyme or reason.

I believe in the power of good food. I believe in the shared experience of a well-prepared meal. And I believe the further we move away from what nature intended for us, the closer we veer towards ill health and despair.

Michelle Obama captured the sentiment well when she reportedly said,

*The problem is when that fun stuff becomes the habit and I think that's what's happened in our culture. Fast food has become the everyday meal.*

Eating well for health is not the quick or easy route. It greatly depends on your point of view. In my home, food is the glue that brings out the best conversations. No meal is eaten away from the dining room or kitchen table, even if I am on my own. It helps that I do not own a television and if I were to eat on the couch, my two dogs would probably steal my food. My meals are planned, the ingredients picked (shopped) by me, and almost every meal is made from scratch. I love the kind of food that tickles my taste buds and makes me feel good. I would rather skip a meal than settle for a sub-optimal offering. This is a conscious choice I have made and so far, my health is proof that it has all been well worth it. I believe that once you have decided to venture on a new path in relation to food, involved the people you spend time with and hold dear, and have seen the improvement in your health, no catchy slogan or fancy advertisement can derail you.

For: One cannot think well, love well, sleep well if one has not dined well. – Virginia Woolf.

# Bibliography

1. ABC news (2016) 'Doctor at Sydney hospital discovers scurvy resurgence due to poor dietary habits',http://www.abc.net.au/news/2016-11-29/resurgence-of-the-rare-condition-of-scurvy-among-diabetics/8073136, accessed on 30 November 2016
2. American College of Gastroenterology (2017), http://patients.gi.org/topics/constipation-and-defection-problems/ accessed 24 February 2017
3. Andreas, C. and Andreas, S. (1989) 'Chapter 12: The Naturally Slender Eating Strategy', in *Heart of the Mind*, Utah, U.S.A., Real People Press, ISBN 0-911226-31-1
4. Arola, L., Bonet, M.L., Delzenne, N., Duggal, M.S., Gómez-Candela, C., Huyghebaert, A., Laville, M., Lingström, P., Livingstone, B., Palou, A., Picó, C., Sanders, T., Schaafsma, G., van Baak, M., van Loveren, C., and van Schothorst, E.M. (2009) 'Summary and general conclusions/outcomes on the role and fate of sugars in human nutrition and health', *Obesity Reviews 2009*; 10, Suppl. 1, pp. 55–58
5. Attaman, J.A., Toth, T.L., Furtado, J., Campos, H., Hauser, R. and Chavarro, J.E. (2012) 'Dietary fat and semen quality among men attending a fertility clinic', *Reproductive epidemiology*, Vol. 27, No. 5, pp. 1466–1474
6. Benecol (2017) http://www.benecol.co.uk/benecol-works?utm_medium=cpc&utm_source=google&utm_term=benecol-cholesterol&utm_content=text&utm_campaign=mec---brand---category---cholesterol-(e)&gclid=CjwKEAjwh9PGBRCfso2n3ODgvUcSJAA

hpW5o5UHgiOrqE8jkP2GHxhHiJnW
1tGM971EAWI8C3UfGZhoCgSnw_wcB&gclsrc=aw.
ds, accessed on 24 March 2017

7.  Bomhof-Roordink, H., Seldenrijk, A., Van Hout, H.P.J., Van Marwijk, H.W.J., Diamant, M. and Penninx, B.W.J.H. (2015) 'Associations between life stress and subclinical cardiovascular disease are partly mediated by depressive and anxiety symptoms', *Journal of Psychosomatic Research*, Vol. 78, pp. 332–339

8.  Britsh Heart Foundation (2013), http://www.bhf.org.uk/heart-health/preventing-heart-disease/healthy-eating.aspx, accessed on 16 July 2013

9.  Bussell, G. (1998) 'Pre-menstrual Syndrome and Diet', *Journal of Nutritional & Environmental Medicine*, 8, pp. 65–75

10. Carding, S., Verbeke, K., Vipond, D.T., Corfe, B.M. and Owen, L.J. (2015) 'Dysbiosis of the gut microbiota in disease', *Microbial Ecology in Health and Disease*, Vol. 26, pp. 1–9

11. Caroli, A., Poli, A., Ricotta, D., Banfi, G. and Cocchi, D (2011) 'Invited review: Dairy intake and bone health: A viewpoint from the state of the art', *Journal of Dairy Science*, Vol. 94, pp. 5249–5262

12. Charmaz, K. (1983) 'Loss of self: A fundamental from of suffering in the chronically ill',

13. *Sociology of Health & Illness*, Vol.5, Issue 2, pp. 168–195

14. Chirila, I., Petrtiu, F.D., Ciortescu, I., Mihai, C. and Drug, V.L. (2012) 'Diet and Irritable Bowel Syndrome', *J Gastroentestin Liver Dis*, Vol. 21, No. 4, pp. 357–362

15. Clark, H. (2011) *The Cure for All Diseases*, California, U.S.A., New Century Press, ISBN 1-890035-01-3

16. Clarkson, P.M. (1993) 'Nutritional ergogenic aids: caffeine, *Int J Sport Nutr.* Vol. 3, pp. 103–111

17. Compton, G. (2017) 'Skinny Mini Desserts — Strawberry Cheesecake', available at https:// skinnyms.com/skinny-mini-strawberry-cheesecake/, accessed 5 October 2017

18. Conlon, M.A. and Bird, A.R. (2015) 'The Impact of Diet and Lifestyle on Gut Microbiota and Human Health', *Nutrient*, Vol. 7, pp. 17–44

19. Department of health (1999) *Dietary Reference Values for Food Energy and Nutrients for the United Kingdom*, London, The Stationery Office.

20. Dr Hulda Clark Professional Zappers (2017), http://drclark.co/uk/, accessed on 24 March 2017

21. Dulwich Health (2017) 'Oxygen Healing Therapy', http://dulwichhealth.co.uk/health-suggestions/oxygen-healing-therapy-oxytech/?v=79cba1185463, accessed on 24 March 2017

22. Fleet, J.S. and Schoch, R.D. (2010) 'Molecular mechanisms for regulation of intestinal calcium absorption by vitamin D and other factors. *Critical Reviews in Clinical Laboratory Sciences*, 47(4), pp. 181–195

23. Food and Agriculture Organisation of the United Nations (2017) 'Buckwheat', http:// www.fao.org/traditional-crops/buckwheat/en/

24. Food and Agriculture Organisation of the United Nations (2015) 'FAO Statistical Pocketbook, Coffee', available at http://www.fao.org/3/a-i4985e.pdf

25. Food Standards Agency (2001) McCance and Widdowson's The Composition of Foods, Fifth edition. Cambridge: Royal Society Chemistry. ISBN 0-85186-391-4

26. Fox, B.A. and Cameron, A.G. (1995) *Food Science, Nutrition & Health*, 6th Edition, London, Edward Arnold

27. Frank, R.T. (1931) 'The Hormonal Causes of Premenstrual Tension', *Arch. of Neur. and Psychiatry*, Vol. 26, No. 5.

28. Greenfield, R.H. (2011) 'An Honest Response – Placebos and IBS', *Alternative Medicine Alert*, Vol. 14, Issue 2, p. 20

29. Grohol, J.M. (2013) 'Top 25 Psychiatric Medication Prescriptions for 2013', available at https://psychcentral.com/lib/top-25-psychiatric-medication-prescriptions-for-2013/

30. He, F.J. and MacGregor, G.A. (2010) 'Reducing population salt intake worldwide: from evidence to implementation', *Progress in Cardiovascular Diseases,* Vol. 52, pp. 363–82

31. Helander, F.H. and Fandriks, L. (2014) 'Surface area of the digestive tracts – revisited',

32. *Scandinavian Journal of Gastroenterology*, Vol. 49, pp. 681–689

33. Henderson, L., Gregory, J. and Swan, G. (2002) *The National Diet and Nutrition Survey: Adults Aged 19–64 Years Types and Quantities of Food Consumed*, Volume 1, The Stationery Office, London

34. Institute of Medicine of the National Academies (2004) *Infant Formula. Evaluating the safety of new ingredients*, Washington, D.C., The National Academies Press, available at https://www.ncbi.nlm.nih.gov/books/NBK215846/pdf/Bookshelf_NBK215846.pdf

35. International Statistical Classification of Diseases and Related Health Problems (2012), https://www.cihi.ca/en/icd_volume_one_2012_en.pdf

36. Johnson, L. (2015) 'Healthy Vegan Avocado Chocolate Mousse', available at http://helloglow.co/healthy-vegan-avocado-chocolate-mousse/, accessed 5 October 2017

37. Joyce, T. and Gibney, M.J. (2008) The impact of added sugar consumption in overall quality in Irish children and teenagers. *Journal of Human Nutrition and Dietetics*. 21, p 438

38. Kotsirilis, V., Vitetta, L., and Sali, A. (2011) *A guide to evidence-based integrative and complementary medicine*, Australia, Churchill Livingstone

39. Kulendra, N. (2014) 'Gastric dilatation and volvulus, *Veterinary Ireland Journal*, Vol. 4, No. 5, pp. 270–273, available at http://www.veterinaryirelandjournal.com/files/sa_may_2014.pdf

40. La Nuova Piramide Della Dieta Mediterranea (2016), http://www.pastazara.it/it/piramide-alimentare-dieta-mediterranea/, accessed on 13 June 2017

41. Lappinga, P.J., Abraham, S.C., Murray, J.A., Vetter, E.A., Patel, R. and Wu, T. (2010) 'Small Intestinal Bacterial Overgrowth', *Arch Pathol Lab Med*, Vol. 134, pp. 264–270

42. Liska, D.J. (2002) 'The Role of Detoxification in the Prevention of Chronic Degenerative Diseases', *Applied Nutritional Science Reports*, Vol. 650, pp. 1–8

43. Lombardi, I., Luisi, S., Quirici, B., Moteleone, P., Bernardi, F., Liut, M., Casarosa, E., Palumbo, M., Petraglia, F. and Genazzani, A.R. (2004) 'Adrenal response to adrenocorticotropic hormone stimulation in patients with premenstrual syndrome', *Genaecol Endocrinol*, Vol. 18, pp. 79–87

44. LoPiccolo, M.C. and Lim, H.W. (2010) Vitamin D in health and disease.

45. *Photodermatology, Photoimmunology & Photomedicine*, Vol. 26, pp. 224–229

46. Ma, Y., Chiriboga, D.E., Olendzki, B.C., Li, W., Leung, K., and Hafner, A.R. (2006) 'Association between Carbohydrate Intake and Serum Lipids', *J Am Coll Nutr*, Vol. 25, Issue 2, pp. 155–163

47. Matini, L. and Ogden, J. (2016), 'A qualitative study of patients' experience of living with inflammatory bowel disease: A preliminary focus on the notion of adaptation', *Journal of Health Psychology*, Vol. 21, Issue 11, pp. 2493–2502

48. Maughan, R.M. (2000), *Nutrition in sport*, Blackwell Science, Oxford, ISBN 0-632-05094-2

49. McGee, H. (2004). *Food & Cooking*. Hodder & Stoughton, London, Chapter 12. ISBN 978-0-340-83149-6

50. Murray, MT (1996) *Encyclopedia of Nutritional Supplements*, California, Prima Publishing

51. National Eye Institute (2017), 'Facts About Age-Related Macular Degeneration', https:// nei.nih.gov/health/maculardegen/armd_facts accessed on 24 April 2017

52. National Human Genome Research Institute, https://www.genome.gov/10001772/

53. Nehra, D., Le, H.D., Fallon, E.M., Carlson, S.J., Woods, D., White, Y.A., Pan, A.H., Guo, L., Rodig, S.J., Tilly, J.L., Rueda, B.R. and Puder, M. (2012) 'Prolonging the female reproductive lifespan and improving egg quality with dietary omega-3 fatty acids', *Aging Cell*, Vol. 11, pp. 1046–1054

54. The New World Encyclopaedia, http://www.newworldencyclopedia.org/entry/Small_int estine

55. NHS choices, Vitamins and minerals – Calcium, http://www.nhs.uk/Conditions/vitamins-minerals/Pages/Calcium.aspx accessed on 2 April 2013

56. Norgine Pharmaceuticals (2017), http://www.norgine.com/about-us/key-facts

57. Nutrition data (2013), http://nutritiondata.self.com/

58. Pizzorno, J.E.Jr., Murray, M.T. and Joiner-Bey, H (2002) *The Clinician's Handbook of Natural Medicine*, Churchill Livingstone, China, ISBN 0-443-07080-6

59. Physicians Committee (2016), Food for Life Cancer Project, https://www.pcrm.org/health/ cancer-resources/diet-cancer/nutrition/how-fiber-helps-protect-against-cancer

60. Reddy, K.R. and Gilchrest, B.A. (2010) Vitamin D Sufficiency vs. Sun Protection: Must We Choose? *Dermatology Nursing*, pp. 2–10

61. Reiffel, J.A. and McDonald, A. (2006) 'Antiarrhythmic effects of omega-3 fatty acids', *AM J Cardiol*, Vol. 98, Issue 4, Supplement 1, pp. 50–60

62. Report on Health and Social Subjects 41 *Dietary Reference Values (DRVs) for Food Energy and Nutrients for the UK*, Report of the Panel on DRVs of the Committee on Medical Aspects of Food Policy (COMA) 1991. The Stationary Office. London. ISBN 0-11-321397-2

63. Richardson, A. (2006) *They are what you feed them*, Harper Thorsons, London, ISBN 978-0-00-718225-1

64. Ruxton, C.H.S., Gardner, E.J., and McNulty, E.M. (2010). Is Sugar Consumption Detrimental to Health? A review of the Evidence 1995–2006. *Food Science and Nutrition*. 50:13

65. Sachdeva, S., Rawat, A.K. and Puri, A.S. (2011) 'Small intestinal bacterial overgrowth (SIBO) in irritable bowel syndrome: Frequency and predictors', *Journal of Gastroenterology and Hepatology*, Vol. 26, Supplement 3, pp. 135–138

66. Sharma, A. (2017) 'An Obesity Manifesto: Debunking the Myths', *Medscape*

67. Sobas, K., Wadolowska, L., Slowinska,. M.A., Czlapka-Matyasik, M. and Niedzwiedzka, E. (2010) 'Analysis of the occurrence of dietary and non-dietary factors of fracture risk in relation to bone mineral density in women', *Acte Sci. Pol. Techno. Aliment*, Vol. 9, Issue 3, pp. 373–382

68. Starbucks (2017), https://www.starbucks.com/menu

69. Stewart, A.C. (1996) 'Effects of nutritional programmes on premenstrual syndrome and work efficiency, *Complement Ther Med*, 1: 68–72

70. Tang, J. and Chonchol, M.B. (2013) 'Vitamin D and Kidney Stone Disease', *Curr Opin Nephrol Hypertens*, Vol. 22, Issue 4, pp. 383–389

71. The Observatory of Economic Complexity (2017), http://atlas.media.mit.edu/en/profile/sitc/2225/#Importers

72. Theobald, H.E. (2005) *Dietary calcium and health*, British Nutrition Foundation, London, UK, pp. 237–277

73. Tortora, G.J. and Derrickson, B. (2000) *Introduction to the Human Body the essentials of anatomy and physiology*, 9th Ed, John Wiley & Sons Inc., New York, ISBN 0-471-69123-2

74. Triggs, C.M., Munday, K., Hu, R., Fraser, A.G., Gearry, R.B., Barclay, M.L. and Ferguson,

75. L.R. (2010) 'Dietary factors in chronic inflammation: Food tolerances and intolerances of a New Zealand Caucasian Crohn's disease population', *Mutation Research*, Vol. 690, pp. 123–138

76. WHO (2013), http://www.who.int/mediacentre/factsheets/fs312/en/

77. WHO (2014) 'WHA Global Nutrition Targets 2025: Anaemia Policy Brief',

http://www.who.int/nutrition/topics/globaltargets_anaemia_policybrief.pdf?ua=1

78. WHO (2016)
http://www.who.int/dietphysicalactivity/fruit/en/

79. Willis, K.S., Peterson, N.J. and Larson-Meyer, D.E. (2008) 'Should We Be Concerned About the Vitamin D Status of Athletes?' *International Journal of Sport Nutrition and Exercise Metabolism*, Vol. 18, pp. 204–224

80. Withrow, D. and Alter, D.A. (2011) 'The economic burden of obesity worldwide: a systematic review of the direct costs of obesity.' *Obesity Review*, Vol.12, Issue 2, pp. 131–141

81. Wolraich, M. L., Wilson, D. B. and White, J. W. (1995). The effect of sugar on behavior or cognition in children. A meta-analysis. *JAMA.* **274**:1617–1621.

82. Yoon, S.L., Grundmann, O. and Farrell, L. (2011) 'Management of Irritable Bowel Syndrome (IBS) in Adults: Conventional and Complementary/Alternative Approaches', *Altern Med Rev*, Vol.16, Issue 2, pp. 134–151

83. Zaka, M. and Mahmood, K.T. (2012) 'Pre-menstrual syndrome – a review', *Journal of Phamaceutical Sciences and Research*, Vol. 4, No.1, pp. 1684–1691

84. Zeng, H., Lazarova, D.L. and Bordonaro, M. (2015) 'Mechanisms linking dietary fiber, gut microbiota and colon cancer prevention', *World Journal of Gatrointestinal Oncology*, Vol. 6, Issue 2, pp. 41–51

85. Zhang, P., Zhang, X., Brown, J., Vistisen, D., Sicree, R., Shaw, J. and Nichols, G. (2010) 'Global healthcare expenditure on diabetes for 2010 and 2030', *Diabetes Research and Clinical Practice*, Vol. 87, pp. 293–301

86. Zhang, R. and Naughton, D.P. (2010) 'Vitamin D in health and disease: Current perspectives', *Nutrition Journal*, 9:65

87. Zietal, B. (2016) 'The Genesis of Premenstrual Syndrome', *Arizona State University,* Thesis for Master of Science degree, available at
https://repository.asu.edu/attachments/
170732/content/Zietal_asu_0010N_16153.pdf